Oklahoma BIRDS

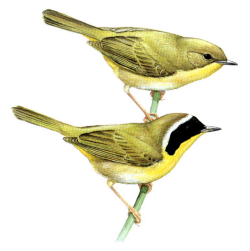

*Ted Cable, Scott Seltman,
Krista Kagume & Gregory Kennedy*

Lone Pine Publishing International

This book is dedicated to the memory of Oklahoma birder and naturalist Bob Jennings.

© 2007 by Lone Pine Publishing International Inc.
First printed in 2007   10 9 8 7 6 5 4 3 2 1
Printed in China

All rights reserved. No part of this work covered by the copyrights hereon may be reproduced or used in any form or by any means—graphic, electronic or mechanical—without the prior written permission of the publisher, except for reviewers, who may quote brief passages. Any request for photocopying, recording, taping or storage on information retrieval systems of any part of this work shall be directed in writing to the publisher.

The Distributor: Lone Pine Publishing
1808 B Street NW, Suite 140
Auburn, WA, USA 98001

Website: www.lonepinepublishing.com

Library and Archives Canada Cataloguing in Publication

Compact guide to Oklahoma birds / Ted T. Cable ... [et al.].

Includes bibliographical references and index.
ISBN 978-976-8200-23-5

1. Birds--Oklahoma--Identification. I. Cable, Ted T.

QL684.O5C64 2007   598'.09766   C2006-906333-8

Illustrations: Gary Ross, Ted Nordhagen, Eva Pluciennik
Digital Scanning: Elite Lithographers Co.
Egg Photography: Allan Bibby, Gary Whyte

We wish to thank the Royal Alberta Museum for providing access to their egg collections.

PC: P13

Contents

Reference Guide.................... 4 *Introduction*...................... 10

Geese, Ducks..	20
Pheasants, Turkeys, Quails..	40
Grebes, Gannets, Cormorants	46
Herons, Egrets, Vultures	52
Kites, Eagles, Hawks, Kestrels	60
Coots	74
Plovers, Sandpipers	76
Gulls, Terns..	84
Pigeons, Doves, Cuckoos, Roadrunners	90
Owls	100
Nightjars, Swifts, Hummingbirds, Kingfishers........	106
Woodpeckers, Flickers..	114
Flycatchers, Kingbirds	122
Shrikes...	134
Jays, Crows..	136
Larks, Martins, Swallows..	140
Chickadees, Titmice, Nuthatches, Wrens	148
Kinglets, Bluebirds, Robins.......................................	158
Catbirds, Mockingbirds, Starlings, Waxwings	164
Warblers, Yellowthroats, Tanagers	174
Sparrows, Cardinals, Buntings.................................	184
Blackbirds, Meadowlarks, Cowbirds, Orioles	212
Finches, Goldfinches, Old World Sparrows..............	222

Glossary............................... 230 *Checklist*.......................... 232
Index 238

4 Reference Guide

WATERFOWL

Snow Goose
size 42 in • p. 20

Canada Goose
size 42 in • p. 22

Wood Duck
size 17 in • p. 24

Gadwall
size 20 in • p. 26

Mallard
size 24 in • p. 28

Blue-winged Teal
size 14 in • p. 30

Redhead
size 20 in • p. 32

Lesser Scaup
size 16 in • p. 34

Common Goldeneye
size 18 in • p. 36

GROUSELIKE BIRDS & QUAILS

Common Merganser
size 24 in • p. 38

Ring-necked Pheasant
size 34 in • p. 40

Wild Turkey
size 40 in • p. 42

DIVING BIRDS

Northern Bobwhite
size 10 in • p. 44

Pied-billed Grebe
size 13 in • p. 46

American White Pelican
size 60 in • p. 48

HERONS & VULTURES

Double-crested Cormorant
size 29 in • p. 50

Great Blue Heron
size 51 in • p. 52

Great Egret
size 39 in • p. 54

Reference Guide 5

Black-crowned Night-Heron
size 24 in • p. 56

Turkey Vulture
size 28 in • p. 58

Mississippi Kite
size 14 in • p. 60

Bald Eagle
size 36 in • p. 62

Northern Harrier
size 20 in • p. 64

Cooper's Hawk
size 18 in • p. 66

Swainson's Hawk
size 20 in • p. 68

Red-tailed Hawk
size 21 in • p. 70

American Kestrel
size 8 in • p. 72

American Coot
size 14 in • p. 74

Killdeer
size 10 in • p. 76

Spotted Sandpiper
size 7 in • p. 78

Lesser Yellowlegs
size 10 in • p. 80

Baird's Sandpiper
size 7 in • p. 82

Franklin's Gull
size 14 in • p. 84

Ring-billed Gull
size 19 in • p. 86

Forster's Tern
size 15 in • p. 88

Rock Pigeon
size 12 in • p. 90

HERONS & VULTURES | **BIRDS OF PREY** | **COOTS** | **SHOREBIRDS** | **GULLS & TERNS** | **DOVES & CUCKOOS**

6 Reference Guide

DOVES & CUCKOOS

Eurasian Collared-Dove
size 12 in • p. 92

Mourning Dove
size 12 in • p. 94

Yellow-billed Cuckoo
size 12 in • p. 96

OWLS

Greater Roadrunner
size 23 in • p. 98

Eastern Screech-Owl
size 8 in • p. 100

Great Horned Owl
size 21 in • p. 102

NIGHTJARS & HUMMINGBIRDS

Barred Owl
size 20 in • p. 104

Common Nighthawk
size 9 in • p. 106

Chimney Swift
size 5 in • p. 108

Ruby-throated Hummingbird
size 4 in • p. 110

Belted Kingfisher
size 12 in • p. 112

Red-headed Woodpecker
size 12 in • p. 114

WOODPECKERS

Red-bellied Woodpecker
size 10 in • p. 116

Downy Woodpecker
size 6 in • p. 118

Northern Flicker
size 12 in • p. 120

FLYCATCHERS

Least Flycatcher
size 5 in • p. 122

Eastern Phoebe
size 7 in • p. 124

Great Crested Flycatcher
size 8 in • p. 126

Reference Guide 7

FLYCATCHERS

Western Kingbird
size 8 in • p. 128

Eastern Kingbird
size 9 in • p. 130

Scissor-tailed Flycatcher
size 10 in • p. 132

SHRIKES, JAYS & CROWS

Loggerhead Shrike
size 9 in • p. 134

Blue Jay
size 11 in • p. 136

American Crow
size 19 in • p. 138

LARKS & SWALLOWS

Horned Lark
size 7 in • p. 140

Purple Martin
size 7 in • p. 142

Cliff Swallow
size 5 in • p. 144

Barn Swallow
size 7 in • p. 146

Carolina Chickadee
size 4 in • p. 148

Tufted Titmouse
size 6 in • p. 150

CHICKADEES, NUTHATCHES & WRENS

White-breasted Nuthatch
size 6 in • p. 152

Carolina Wren
size 5 in • p. 154

House Wren
size 5 in • p. 156

KINGLETS & THRUSHES

Golden-crowned Kinglet
size 4 in • p. 158

Eastern Bluebird
size 7 in • p. 160

American Robin
size 10 in • p. 162

8 Reference Guide

MIMICS, STARLINGS & WAXWINGS

Gray Catbird
size 9 in • p. 164

Northern Mockingbird
size 10 in • p. 166

Brown Thrasher
size 11 in • p. 168

European Starling
size 8 in • p. 170

Cedar Waxwing
size 7 in • p. 172

Orange-crowned Warbler
size 5 in • p. 174

WOOD-WARBLERS & TANAGERS

Yellow Warbler
size 5 in • p. 176

Yellow-rumped Warbler
size 5 in • p. 178

Common Yellowthroat
size 5 in • p. 180

Summer Tanager
size 7 in • p. 182

Spotted Towhee
size 7 in • p. 184

American Tree Sparrow
size 6 in • p. 186

SPARROWS & BUNTINGS

Chipping Sparrow
size 5 in • p. 188

Lark Sparrow
size 6 in • p. 190

Grasshopper Sparrow
size 5 in • p. 192

Song Sparrow
size 6 in • p. 194

Harris's Sparrow
size 7 in • p. 196

Reference Guide 9

SPARROWS, CARDINALS & BUNTINGS

White-crowned Sparrow
size 6 in • p. 198

Dark-eyed Junco
size 6 in • p. 200

Lapland Longspur
size 6 in • p. 202

Northern Cardinal
size 8 in • p. 204

Indigo Bunting
size 5 in • p. 206

Painted Bunting
size 5 in • p. 208

BLACKBIRDS & ALLIES

Dickcissel
size 6 in • p. 210

Red-winged Blackbird
size 8 in • p. 212

Western Meadowlark
size 9 in • p. 214

Common Grackle
size 12 in • p. 216

Brown-headed Cowbird
size 7 in • p. 218

Baltimore Oriole
size 7 in • p. 220

FINCHLIKE BIRDS

House Finch
size 5 in • p. 222

Pine Siskin
size 5 in • p. 224

American Goldfinch
size 4 in • p. 226

House Sparrow
size 6 in • p. 228

Introduction

If you have ever admired a songbird's pleasant notes, been fascinated by a soaring hawk or wondered about the identity of a songbird at your, this book is for you. There is so much to discover about birds and their surroundings that birding is becoming one of the fastest growing hobbies on the planet. Many people find it relaxing, while others enjoy its outdoor appeal. Some people see it as a way to reconnect with nature, an opportunity to socialize with like-minded people or a way to monitor the environment.

Whether you are just beginning to take an interest in birds or can already identify many species, there is always more to learn. We've highlighted both the remarkable traits and the more typical behaviors displayed by some of our most abundant or noteworthy birds. A few live in specialized habitats, but most are common species that you have a good chance of encountering on most outings or in your backyard.

BIRDING IN OKLAHOMA

We are truly blessed by the geographical and biological diversity of Oklahoma. In addition to supporting a wide range of breeding birds and year-round residents, our state hosts a large number of spring and fall

Northern Cardinal

migrants that move through our area on the way to their breeding and wintering grounds. In all, 470 bird species have been seen and recorded in Oklahoma.

Identifying birds in action and under varying conditions involves skill, timing and luck. The more you know about a bird—its range, preferred habitat, food preferences and hours and seasons of activity—the better your chances will be of seeing it. Generally, spring and fall are the busiest birding times. Temperatures are moderate then, many species of birds are on the move and male songbirds are belting out their unique courtship songs. Birds are usually most active in the early morning hours, except in winter when they forage during the day when milder temperatures prevail.

Another useful clue for correctly recognizing birds is knowledge of their habitat. Simply put, a bird's habitat is the place where it normally lives. Some birds prefer open water, some are found in cattail marshes, others like mature coniferous forest, and still other birds prefer abandoned agricultural fields overgrown with tall grass and shrubs. Habitats are just like neighborhoods: if you associate friends with the suburb in which they live, you can easily learn to associate specific birds with their preferred habitat. Only in migration, especially during inclement weather, do some birds leave their usual habitat.

Recognizing birds by their songs and calls can greatly enhance your birding experience. Numerous tapes and CDs are available to help you learn bird songs, and a portable player with headphones can let you quickly compare a live bird with a recording. The old-fashioned way to remember bird songs is to make up words for them. We have given you some of the classic renderings in the species accounts that follow. Some of these approximations work better than others; birds often add or delete syllables from their calls, and very few pronounce consonants in a recognizable fashion. Remember, too, that songs may vary from place to place.

Oklahoma has a long tradition of friendly, recreational birding. In general, birders are willing to help beginners, share their knowledge and involve novices in their projects. Christmas bird counts, breeding bird surveys, nest box programs, migration monitoring, and birding lectures and workshops provide a chance for birdwatchers of all levels to interact and share the splendor of birds. Bird hotlines provide up-to-date information on the sightings of rarities, which are often easier to relocate than you might think. For more information or to participate in these projects, contact the following organizations:

Audubon Society of Central Oklahoma
www.audubon-society-of-central-ok.org
Publishes *The Kiteflight*

Oklahoma City Audubon Society
www.okc-audubon.org

Oklahoma Ornithological Society
P.O. Box 2931, Claremore, OK 74018
www.okbirds.org

Tulsa Audubon Society
P.O. Box 2476, Tulsa, OK 74101
Phone: (918) 809-6325
www.tulsaaudubon.org
Publishes *Tulsa Scissortail*

BIRD LISTING
Many birders list the species they have seen during excursions or at home. It is up to you to decide what kind of list—systematic or casual—you will keep, and you may choose not to make lists at all. Lists may prove rewarding in unexpected ways, and after you visit a new area, your list becomes a souvenir of your experiences there. Keeping regular, accurate lists of birds in your neighborhood can also be useful for local researchers. It can be interesting to compare the arrival dates and last sightings of hummingbirds and other seasonal visitors, or to note the first sighting of a new visitor to your area.

BIRD FEEDING
Many people set up bird feeders in their backyard, especially in winter. It is possible to attract specific birds by choosing the right kind of food and style of feeder. Keep your feeder stocked through late spring because birds have a hard time finding food before the flowers bloom, seeds develop and insects hatch. Contrary to popular opinion, birds do not become dependent on feeders, nor do they subsequently forget to forage naturally. Be sure to clean your feeder and the surrounding area regularly to prevent the spread of disease.

Landscaping your property with native plants is another way of providing natural food for birds. Flocks of waxwings have a keen eye for red mountain ash berries and hummingbirds enjoy columbine flowers. The cumulative effects of "nature-scaping" urban yards can be a significant step toward habitat conservation (especially when you consider that habitat is often lost in small amounts—a seismic line is cut in one area and a highway is built in another). Many good books and web sites about attracting wildlife to your backyard are available.

NEST BOXES

Another popular way to attract birds is to put up nest boxes, especially for House Wrens, Eastern Bluebirds and Purple Martins. Not all birds will use nest boxes: only species that normally use cavities in trees are comfortable in such confined spaces. Larger nest boxes can attract American Kestrels, screech-owls and Wood Ducks.

CLEANING NEST BOXES AND FEEDERS

Nest boxes and feeding stations must be kept clean to prevent birds from becoming ill or spreading disease. Old nesting material may harbor a number of parasites. Once the birds have left for the season, remove the old nesting material and wash and scrub the nest box with detergent or a 10 percent bleach solution (1 part bleach to 9 parts water). You can also scald the nest box with boiling water. Rinse it well and let it dry thoroughly before you remount it.

Unclean bird feeders can become contaminated with salmonellosis and possibly other diseases. Seed feeders should be cleaned monthly; hummingbird feeders at least weekly. Any seed, fruit or suet that is moldy or spoiled must be discarded. Clean and disinfect feeding stations with a 10 percent bleach solution, scrubbing thoroughly. Rinse the feeder well and allow it to dry completely before refilling it. Discarded seed and feces on the ground under the feeding station should also be removed.

We advise that you wear rubber gloves and a mask when cleaning nest boxes or feeders.

WEST NILE VIRUS

Since the West Nile Virus first surfaced in North America in 1999, it has caused fear and misunderstanding. Some people have become afraid of contracting the disease from birds, and some health departments have advised residents to eliminate feeding stations and birdbaths.

To date, the disease has reportedly killed 284 species of birds. Corvids (crows, jays and ravens) and birds of prey have been the most obvious victims because their size makes it easy to identify their corpses, though the disease also affects some smaller species. The virus is transmitted among birds and to humans (as well as some other mammals) by mosquitoes that have bitten infected birds. Birds do not get the disease directly from other birds, and humans cannot get it from casual contact with infected birds. As well, not all mosquito species can carry the disease. According to the Centers for Disease Control and Prevention (CDC), only about 20 percent of people who are bitten and become infected will develop any symptoms at all, and less than 1 percent will become severely ill.

Because mosquitoes breed in standing water, birdbaths have the potential to become mosquito breeding grounds. Birdbaths should be emptied and the water changed at least weekly. Drippers, circulating pumps, fountains or waterfalls that keep water moving will prevent mosquitoes from laying their eggs in the water. There are also bird-friendly products available to treat water in birdbaths. Contact your local nature store or garden center for more information on these products.

ABOUT THE SPECIES ACCOUNTS

This book gives detailed accounts of 105 species of birds that can be expected in Oklahoma on an annual basis. The order of the birds and their common and scientific names follow the American Ornithologists' Union's *Check-list of North American Birds* (7th edition, July 1998, and its supplements through 2006).

As well as showing the identifying features of the bird, each species account also attempts to bring the bird to life by describing its various character traits. One of the challenges of birding is that many species look different in spring and summer than they do in fall and winter.

Many birds have breeding and nonbreeding plumages, and immature birds often look different from their parents. This book does not try to describe or illustrate all the different plumages of a species; instead, it tries to focus on the forms that are most likely to be seen in our area.

ID: Large illustrations point out prominent field marks that will help you tell each bird apart. The descriptions favor easily understood language instead of technical terms.

Other ID: This section lists additional identifying features. Some of the most common anatomical features of birds are pointed out in the Glossary illustration (p. 231).

Size: The average length of the bird's body from bill to tail, as well as wingspan, are given and are approximate measurements of the bird as it is seen in nature. The size is sometimes given as a range, because there is variation between individuals, or between males and females.

Voice: You will hear many birds, particularly songbirds, which may remain hidden from view. Memorable paraphrases of distinctive sounds will aid you in identifying a species by ear.

Status: A general comment, such as "common," "uncommon" or "rare," is usually sufficient to describe the relative abundance of a species. Situations are bound to vary somewhat since migratory pulses, seasonal changes and centers of activity tend to concentrate or disperse birds.

Habitat: The habitats listed describe where each species is most commonly found. Because of the freedom that flight gives them, birds can turn up in almost any type of habitat. However, they will usually be found in environments that provide the specific food, water, cover and, in some cases, nesting habitat that they need to survive.

Similar Birds: Easily confused species are illustrated for each account. If you concentrate on the most relevant field marks, the subtle differences between species can be reduced to easily identifiable traits. Even experienced birders can mistake one species for another.

Nesting: In each species account, nest location and structure, clutch size, incubation period and parental duties are discussed. A photo of the bird's egg is also provided. Remember that birding ethics discourage the disturbance of active bird nests. If you disturb a nest, you may drive off the parents during a critical period or expose defenseless young to predators.

Range Maps: The range map for each species shows the general overall range of the species in an average year. Most birds will confine their annual movements to this range, although each year some birds wander beyond their traditional boundaries. The maps show year-round, summer and winter ranges, as well as migratory pathways—areas of the region where birds may appear while en route to nesting or winter habitat. The representations of the pathways do not distinguish high-use migration corridors from areas that are seldom used.

Range Map Symbols

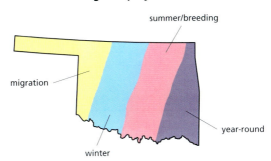

TOP BIRDING SITES

From the cypress bottoms and loblolly pine forests of the eastern part of the state, to the short-grass prairies and mesquite grasslands in the west, Oklahoma can be separated into several natural regions. These regions include the High Plains, Southwestern Tablelands, Central Great Plains, Flint Hills, Cross Timbers, East Central Texas Plains, South Central Plains, Ouachita Mountains, Arkansas Valley, Boston Mountains, Ozark Highlands and Central Irregular Plains. Each region is composed of a number of different habitats that support a wealth of wildlife.

There are hundreds of good birding areas throughout our region. The following areas have been selected to represent a broad range of bird communities and habitats, with an emphasis on accessibility.

1. Black Mesa SP
2. Salt Plains NWR
3. Tallgrass Prairie National Preserve
4. Lake Keystone
5. Oxley Nature Center & Mohawk Park
6. Sequoyah NWR
7. Wichita Mountains NWR
8. Martin Park Nature Center
9. Hackberry Flats
10. Beaver's Bend SP

NWR = National Wildlife Refuge

SP = State Park

Introduction 19

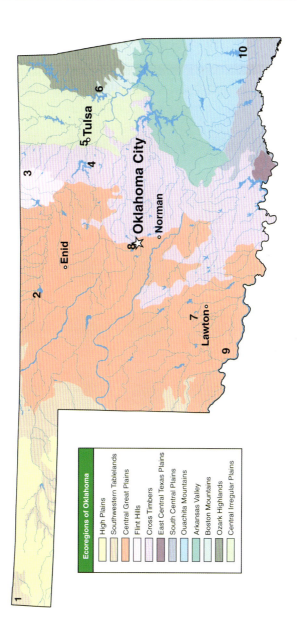

Snow Goose
Chen caerulescens

Noisy flocks of Snow Geese can be quite entertaining, creating a moving patchwork in the sky with their black wing tips and white plumage. • These geese breed in the Arctic and northeastern Siberia, crossing the Bering Strait twice a year. Their smiling, serrated bills are made for grazing on short Arctic tundra and gripping the slippery roots of marsh plants. • Snow Geese can fly at speeds up to 50 miles per hour. They are also strong walkers and mothers have been known to lead their goslings up to 45 miles on foot in search of suitable habitat. • Ross's Goose are smaller versions of the Snow Goose.

Other ID: head often stained rusty red. *Blue morph:* rare; dark blue-gray body.
Size: L 30–33 in; W 4½–5 ft.
Voice: loud, nasal, *houk-houk* in flight, higher pitched and more constant than the Canada Goose's call.
Status: common migrant and winter resident in the east, uncommon in the west.
Habitat: croplands, large rivers and reservoirs.

Similar Birds

Ross's Goose   Tundra Swan   Trumpeter Swan

Snow Goose 21

Nesting: does not nest in Oklahoma; nests in the Arctic; female builds a nest lined with grass, feathers and down; creamy white eggs are 3 1/8 x 2 in; female incubates 4–7 eggs for 22–25 days.

Did You Know?

The Snow Goose has two color morphs, a white and a blue, which until 1983 were considered two different species.

Look For

Snow Geese fly in wavy, disorganized lines whereas Canada Geese fly in V-formation. Occasionally mixed flocks form in migration.

Canada Goose
Branta canadensis

Canada Geese mate for life and are devoted parents. Unlike most birds, the family stays together for nearly a year, which increases the survival rate of the young. Rescuers who care for injured geese report that these birds readily adopt their human caregivers. However, wild geese can be aggressive, especially when defending young or competing for food. Hissing sounds and low, outstretched necks are signs that you should give these birds some space. • The Canada Goose was split into two species in 2004. The larger subspecies are known as Canada Geese, while the smaller subspecies have been renamed Cackling Geese.

Other ID: dark brown upperparts; light brown underparts. *In flight:* flocks fly in V-formation.
Size: *L* 3–4 ft; *W* up to 6 ft.
Voice: loud, familiar *ah-honk*.
Status: common nesting bird except in the far west and southeast; locally abundant migrant and winter resident.
Habitat: lakeshores, riverbanks, ponds, marshes, farmlands and city parks.

Similar Birds

Cackling Goose

Greater White-fronted Goose

Canada Goose 23

long, black neck

white "chin strap"

short, black tail

white undertail coverts

Nesting: usually on the ground; female builds a nest of grass and mud, lined with down; white eggs are 3½ x 2¼ in; female incubates 3–8 eggs for 25–28 days; goslings hatch in May.

Did You Know?

On land, Canada Geese love to eat the new growth of grasses on lawns and golf courses.

Look For

During migration look for Cackling Geese with their smaller bills and smaller overall size among flocks of Canada Geese.

Wood Duck
Aix sponsa

As its name implies, the Wood Duck is a forest-dwelling duck, equipped with fairly sharp claws for perching on branches and nesting in tree cavities. • Female Wood Ducks often return to the same nest site year after year, especially after successfully raising a brood. The young's chance of survival may increase at traditional nest sites, where the adults are familiar with potential threats. If Wood Ducks nest in a local park or farmyard, do not approach the nest because fewer disturbances increase the young's chance of survival.

Other ID: *Male:* glossy, green head with some white streaks; white-spotted, purplish chestnut breast; dark back and hindquarters; long tail. *Female:* gray-brown upperparts; white belly.
Size: *L* 15–20 in; *W* 30 in.
Voice: *Male:* ascending *ter-wee-wee*. *Female:* squeaky *woo-e-e-k*.
Status: uncommon summer resident and migrant; rare winter resident.
Habitat: swamps, ponds, marshes and lakeshores with wooded edges.

Similar Birds

Hooded Merganser

Look For

The male Wood Duck's colorful plumage make it appear as if formally dressed for a wedding, hence its scientific name, *sponsa*, which is Latin for "promised bride."

Wood Duck 25

Nesting: in a hollow, tree cavity or artificial nest box; usually near water; cavity is lined with down; white to buff eggs are 2⅛ x 1⅝ in; female incubates 9–14 eggs for 25–35 days.

Did You Know?

Overharvesting, deforestation and wetland habitat loss seemed likely to drive Wood Ducks to extinction in the late 19th century. However, thousands of nest boxes erected across the Wood Duck's breeding range and hunting restrictions have helped this species recover.

26 Waterfowl

Gadwall
Anas strepera

Gadwall numbers have recently reached record levels, with the North American population climbing to over 1.4 million breeding pairs in the 21st century. These medium-sized dabbling ducks are known for their lack of colorful plumage. Both sexes are grayish brown overall, with bold white wing patches. Males may be identified by their black rump and undertail coverts and females by their orange and brown bills.
• Gadwalls feed on a variety of aquatic plants and invertebrates and are typically found in deeper water, farther from shore than other dabbling ducks.

Other ID: black tail and upper- and undertail coverts. *Male:* dark above; grayish brown head; dark eyes and bill; yellow legs; black breast patch and gray flanks.
Size: *L* 18–22 in; *W* 33 in.
Voice: both sexes quack like a Mallard.
Status: common migrant and winter resident; rare in summer.
Habitat: freshwater lakes or ponds.

Similar Birds

American Wigeon

Mallard
(p. 28)

Northern Pintail

Gadwall

Nesting: well-concealed nest is a grassy, down-lined hollow placed in tall vegetation, sometimes far from water; creamy or pale green eggs are 2¼ x 1½ in; female incubates 8–11 eggs for 24–27 days.

Did You Know?

Gadwalls form monogamous pairs and most females have found a mate by November, long before the nesting season.

Look For

During winter, these ducks commonly feed in association with American Wigeons (*A. americana*) and American Coots.

Mallard
Anas platyrhynchos

The male Mallard, with his shiny green head and chestnut brown breast, is the classic wild duck. Mallards can be seen year-round, often in flocks and always near open water. After breeding, male ducks lose their elaborate plumage, helping them stay camouflaged during their flightless period. In early fall, they molt back into breeding colors. • Female ducks are mostly brown and often hard to tell apart.

Other ID: orange feet. *Male:* white "necklace"; black tail feathers curl upward. *Female:* mottled brown overall. *In flight:* dark blue speculum bordered by white.
Size: *L* 20–28 in; *W* 3 ft.
Voice: quacks; female is louder than male.
Status: abundant migrant and winter resident; uncommon summer resident mostly in the north and west.
Habitat: lakes, wetlands, rivers, city parks, agricultural areas and sewage lagoons.

Similar Birds

Northern Shoveler

American Black Duck

Northern Pintail

Mallard

glossy, green head

yellow bill

orange bill is spattered with black

♂ ♀

Nesting: female builds a grass nest on the ground or under a bush; creamy, grayish or greenish white eggs are 2¼ x 1⅝ in; female incubates 7–10 eggs for 26–30 days.

Did You Know?

A nesting hen generates enough body heat to make the grasses around her nest grow faster. She uses the tall grasses to further conceal her precious nest.

Look For

Mallards will freely hybridize with domestic ducks and American Black Ducks (*A. rubripes*). The resulting offspring are a confusing blend of both parental types.

Blue-winged Teal
Anas discors

Small, speedy Blue-winged Teals are renowned for their aviation skills. They can be identified by their small size and by the sharp twists and turns they execute in flight. • Blue-winged Teals and other dabbling ducks feed by tipping up their tails and dunking their heads underwater. Dabbling ducks have small feet situated near the center of their bodies. Other ducks, such as scaup, goldeneyes and Buffleheads, dive underwater to feed, propelled by large feet set farther back on their bodies.

Other ID: broad, flat bill. *Male:* white undertail coverts. *Female:* mottled brown overall.
Size: *L* 14–16 in; *W* 23 in.
Voice: *Male:* soft *keck-keck-keck*. *Female:* soft quacks.
Status: common migrant; uncommon nesting species mostly in northern counties; rare winter resident in the south.
Habitat: shallow lake edges and wetlands; prefers areas with short but dense emergent vegetation.

Similar Birds

Green-winged Teal Cinnamon Teal

Blue-winged Teal 31

- white throat ♀
- blue-gray head
- white crescent on face ♂
- black-spotted breast and sides

Nesting: nests in the north-central U.S. and Canada; along a grassy shoreline or in a meadow; nest is built with grass and considerable amounts of down; whitish eggs are 1¾ x 1¼ in; female incubates 8–13 eggs for 23–27 days.

Did You Know?

Blue-winged Teals migrate farther than most ducks. They summer as far as the Canadian tundra and overwinter mainly in Central and South America.

Look For

Blue-winged Teals are the first ducks to migrate in the fall—look for them as soon as early September. They begin to arrive again in spring in late March.

Redhead
Aythya americana

The Redhead is a diving duck, but it will occasionally feed on the surface of a wetland like a dabbler.
• Redheads and Canvasbacks have very similar plumage and habitat preferences. The best way to separate the two species is by head shape. The Redhead has a rounded head that meets the bill at an angle, while its close cousin has a sloping forehead that seems to merge with the bill. In males, the most obvious difference between them is the color of their backs—gray in Redheads and white in Canvasbacks.

Other ID: red eyes; short neck. *Female:* warm brown overall, with gray undertones on back and sides; pale throat; usually has pale markings behind and below eyes. *In flight:* relatively slow, shallow wingbeats.
Size: *L* 18–22 in. *W* 27–29 in. (males are larger than females)
Voice: seldom heard away from nesting sites; in courtship, male utters a cat-like *meeow* call; female gives a rolling *kurr-kurr-kurr* and a *squak* alarm.
Status: common migrant; uncommon winter resident; rare summer resident.
Habitat: ponds, lakes and wetlands with vegetated borders.

Similar Birds

Canvasback   Greater Scaup

Redhead

- pale gray hindwing contrasts with darker forewing
- rich rufous-mahogany head and neck
- bluish gray, white-ringed, black-tipped bill
- gray back and sides
- black breast and hindquarters

Nesting: well concealed at the base of emergent vegetation, suspended over water; deep basket of reeds and grass is lined with fine down; creamy white eggs are 2⅜ x 1⅝ in; female incubates 9–13 eggs for 24–28 days.

Did You Know?

Female Redheads may lay their eggs in the nests of other ducks. More than 80 eggs from several females have been found in a "dump nest."

Look For

During migration, Redheads can sometimes be seen among large flocks of Canvasbacks but will also appear among dabbling ducks in urban areas.

Lesser Scaup
Aythya affinis

Male scaup have a bicolored appearance like that of an Oreo cookie—black at both ends and white in the middle—that makes these widespread diving ducks easy to recognize and remember. Two scaup species occur in Oklahoma and are most reliably separated by the amount of white in the wing, a fieldmark usually seen only in flight. The Lesser Scaup has a smaller, white inner wing stripe that changes to dull gray on its primaries, while the Greater Scaup has a larger white wing stripe that extends out into the primary flight feathers.

Other ID: small to medium-sized diving duck; gray-blue bill with a black "nail"; yellow eyes; highest point of head is above and behind eye. *Male:* dark-tipped, white flank feathers; grayish back. *Female:* dark brown.
Size: *L* 15–18 in; *W* 25 in.
Voice: generally silent in winter; alarm call is a deep *scaup*.
Status: common migrant; uncommon winter resident.
Habitat: lakes, open marshes and along slow-moving rivers.

Similar Birds

Greater Scaup

Ring-necked Duck

Lesser Scaup 35

Nesting: does not nest in Oklahoma; nests in northwestern states, Canada and Alaska; in tall, concealing vegetation, generally close to water; nest hollow is built of grass and lined with down; olive buff eggs are 2¼ x 1½ in; female incubates 8–10 eggs for about 25 days.

Did You Know?

The name "scaup" might be a phonetic imitation of one of its calls.

Look For

A member of the *Aythya* genus of diving ducks, the Lesser Scaup leaps up neatly before diving underwater, where it propels itself with powerful strokes of its feet.

Common Goldeneye
Bucephala clangula

The Common Goldeneye typically spends its entire life in North America, dividing its time between breeding grounds in the boreal forests of Canada and Alaska and its winter territory in marine bays and estuaries along the Atlantic and Pacific coasts. Many goldeneyes also overwinter on large inland rivers, lakes and reservoirs, but their numbers depend on food availability and open water. • Fish, crustaceans and mollusks make up a major portion of the Common Goldeneye's winter diet, but in summer, this diving duck eats aquatic invertebrates and tubers.

Other ID: golden eyes. *Male:* dark bill; dark, iridescent, green head; dark back; white sides and belly. *Female:* lighter breast and belly; gray-brown body plumage; dark bill is tipped with yellow in spring and summer.
Size: *L* 16–20 in; *W* 26 in.
Voice: generally silent in migration and winter.
Status: common winter resident.
Habitat: open water of lakes, large ponds and rivers.

Similar Birds

Bufflehead

Barrow's Goldeneye

Common Goldeneye 37

Nesting: does not nest in Oklahoma; nests in Canada and Alaska; in a tree cavity or occasionally a nest box lined with wood chips and down; often close to water; blue-green eggs are 2⅜ x 1⅝ in; female incubates 6–10 eggs for 28–32 days.

Did You Know?

In winter, female Common Goldeneyes fly farther south than males, and juvenile birds continue even farther south.

Look For

Common Goldeneyes are frequently called "Whistlers," because the wind whistles through their wings when they fly.

Common Merganser
Mergus merganser

Lumbering like a jumbo jet, the Common Merganser must run along the surface of the water, beating its heavy wings to gain sufficient lift to take off. Once up and away, this large duck flies arrow-straight and low over the water, making broad, sweeping turns to follow the meandering shorelines of rivers and lakes. • Common Mergansers are highly social and often gather in large groups during migration. In winter, any source of open water with a fish-filled shoal will support good numbers of these skilled divers. • Two close relatives also visit Oklahoma, the Red-breasted Merganser and the Hooded Merganser.

Other ID: large, elongated body. *Male:* white body plumage; black stripe on back; dark eyes; blood red feet. *Female:* gray body; orangy eyes. *In flight:* shallow wingbeats; body is compressed and arrowlike.
Size: *L* 22–27 in; *W* 34 in.
Voice: *Male:* harsh *uig-a,* like a guitar twang. *Female:* harsh *karr karr.*
Status: common to abundant winter resident.
Habitat: large rivers and lakes.

Similar Birds

Red-breasted Merganser

Hooded Merganser

Common Loon

Common Merganser 39

glossy, green head without crest

blood red bill

rusty neck and crested head

orange bill

clean white chin and breast

Nesting: does not nest in Oklahoma; nests in Canada and western U.S.; in a tree cavity; occasionally on the ground, on a cliff ledge or in a large nest box; usually close to water; pale buff eggs are 2½ x 1¾ in; female incubates 8–11 eggs for 30–35 days.

Did You Know?

The Common Merganser is the most widespread and abundant merganser in North America. It also occurs in Europe and Asia.

Look For

In flight, the Common Merganser has shallow wing beats and an arrowlike, compressed body.

Ring-necked Pheasant
Phasianus colchicus

The Ring-necked Pheasant was brought to North America from China in the late 1800s and was introduced to Oklahoma early in the 20th century. It soon became quite abundant, especially in the arid west, and is today considered to be our most desirable game bird. • Unlike native grouse, the Ring-necked Pheasant does not have feathered legs and feet for insulation. It cannot live on native plants alone and depends on grain and corn crops for survival during severe winters.

Other ID: *Male:* bronze underparts. *Female:* mottled brown overall; light underparts.
Size: *Male:* L 30–36 in; W 31 in. *Female:* L 20–26 in; W 28 in.
Voice: *Male:* loud, raspy, roosterlike crowing: *ka-squawk;* whirring of the wings mostly just before sunrise.
Status: common in northwestern Oklahoma.
Habitat: shrubby grasslands, hayfields, grassy ditches and occasionally croplands; fencelines and woodlots.

Similar Birds

Greater Prairie-Chicken

Greater Roadrunner (p. 98)

Ring-necked Pheasant 41

- naked, red face patch
- green head
- white collar
- large, long, barred tail
- ♂

Nesting: on the ground, among vegetation or next to a log or other natural debris; in a slight depression lined with grass and leaves; olive buff eggs are 1¾ x 1⅜ in; female incubates 10–12 eggs for 23–28 days.

Did You Know?

The Ring-necked Pheasant does not fly long distances; it exhibits bursts of labored flight and then long glides that allows it to escape most predators.

Look For

These birds are a familiar sight along rural roads, usually in small groups.

Wild Turkey
Meleagris gallopavo

The Wild Turkey was once common throughout most of eastern North America, but in the early 20th century, habitat loss and overhunting almost eliminated this bird from Oklahoma except in the extreme southeast. • This charismatic bird is the only native North American animal that has been widely domesticated. The wild ancestors of most domestic animals came from Europe. • Early in life both male and female turkeys gobble. The females eventually outgrow this practice, leaving the males to gobble competitively for the honor of mating.

Other ID: largely unfeathered legs. *Male:* red wattles; black-tipped breast feathers. *Female:* smaller; blue-gray head; less iridescent body; brown-tipped breast feathers.
Size: *Male:* L 3–3½ ft; W 5½ ft. *Female:* L 3 ft; W 4 ft.
Voice: courting male gobbles loudly; alarm call is a loud *pert;* contact call is a loud *keouk-keouk-keouk.*
Status: common year-round resident.
Habitat: deciduous, mixed and riparian woodlands; occasionally in farm fields in late fall and winter.

Similar Birds

Ring-necked Pheasant
(p. 40)

Look For

Eastern Wild Turkeys were reintroduced in eastern Oklahoma, but the Rio Grande race was stocked in western Oklahoma; hybrids thrive in central Oklahoma.

Wild Turkey 43

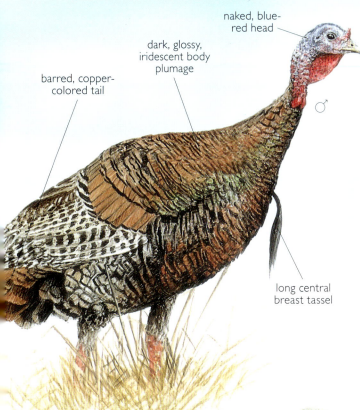

- naked, blue-red head
- dark, glossy, iridescent body plumage
- barred, copper-colored tail
- long central breast tassel
- ♂

Nesting: under thick cover in a woodland or at a field edge; in a depression on the ground, lined with vegetation; brown-speckled, pale buff eggs are 2½ x 1¾ in; female incubates 10–12 eggs for up to 28 days.

Did You Know?

If Congress had taken Benjamin Franklin's advice in 1782, our national emblem would be the Wild Turkey instead of the Bald Eagle. In a letter to his daughter, he wrote that the Bald Eagle was "of bad moral character" while the Wild Turkey was a more honest bird and a true native of America.

Northern Bobwhite
Colinus virginianus

The characteristic whistled *bob-white* call is heard throughout Oklahoma in spring. The male's well-known call is often the only evidence of this bird's presence among the dense, tangled vegetation of its rural, woodland home. • Throughout fall and winter, Northern Bobwhites typically travel in large family groups called coveys. When a predator approaches, the covey bursts into flight, creating a confusing flurry of activity. With the arrival of summer, breeding pairs break away from their coveys to perform elaborate courtship rituals in preparation for another nesting season.

Other ID: mottled brown, buff and black upperparts; short tail.
Size: *L* 10 in; *W* 13 in.
Voice: whistled *hoy* is given year-round. *Male:* a whistled, rising *bob-white* in spring and summer.
Status: common resident year-round.
Habitat: farmlands, open woodlands, woodland edges, grassy fencelines, roadside ditches and brushy, open country.

Similar Birds

Scaled Quail

Look For

Bobwhites benefit from habitat disturbance and are often found in the early succession habitats created by fire, agriculture and forestry.

Northern Bobwhite 45

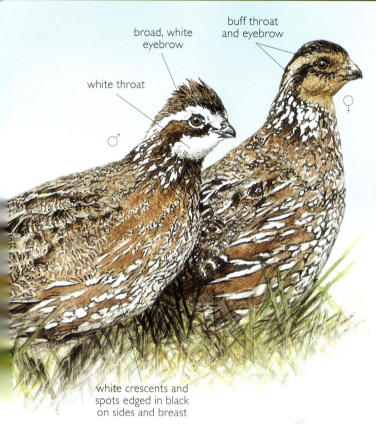

buff throat and eyebrow

broad, white eyebrow

white throat

♂

♀

white crescents and spots edged in black on sides and breast

Nesting: in a shallow depression on the ground, often concealed by vegetation or a woven, partial dome; nest is lined with grass and leaves; white to pale buff eggs are 1¼ x 1 in; pair incubates 12–16 eggs for 22–24 days.

Did You Know?

Northern Bobwhites usually roost in coveys on the ground, huddled together in a circle with each bird facing outward. This enables the group to conserve energy on cold winter nights and to detect danger from any direction. Northern Bobwhites may also roost in shrubs and tangled vines that are above ground.

Pied-billed Grebe
Podilymbus podiceps

Relatively solid bones and the ability to partially deflate its air sac allows the Pied-billed Grebe to sink below the surface of the water like a tiny submarine. The inconspicuous grebe can float low in the water or submerge with only its nostrils and eyes showing above the surface. It will sometimes hide in this way to escape danger, though generally it aggressively chases grebes and other species as part of its territorial defense. The Pied-bill Grebe also keeps a low profile by migrating at night, and landing on the nearest body of water just at or before dawn.

Other ID: *Breeding:* white undertail coverts; pale belly; very short tail. *Nonbreeding:* bill lacks black ring; white chin and throat; brownish crown.
Size: *L* 12–15 in; *W* 16 in.
Voice: loud, whooping call begins quickly, then slows down: *kuk-kuk-kuk cow cow cow cowp cowp cowp*.
Status: common migrant; rare in summer and winter.
Habitat: ponds, marshes and backwaters with sparse emergent vegetation.

Similar Birds

Eared Grebe   Horned Grebe   Western Grebe

Pied-billed Grebe

- dark eye with pale eye ring
- black ring on pale, thick bill
- all-brown body
- black throat

breeding

Nesting: in a wetland; floating platform nest of decaying plants is anchored to emergent vegetation; white to buff eggs are 1⅝ x 1¼ in; pair incubates 4–5 eggs for about 23 days and raises the striped young together.

Did You Know?

An incubating bird frightened by an intruder will cover its eggs and slide underwater, leaving a nest that looks like nothing more than a mat of debris.

Look For

Dark plumage, small size, individually webbed toes and a chickenlike bill distinguish the Pied-billed Grebe from other waterfowl.

American White Pelican
Pelecanus erythrorhynchos

This majestic wetland bird is one of only a few bird species that feeds cooperatively. A group of pelicans will herd fish into a school, and then dip their bucketlike bills into the water to capture their prey. In a single scoop, a pelican can trap over three gallons of water and fish in its bill, which is about two to three times as much as its stomach can hold. This impressive feat inspired Dixon Lanier Merritt to write: "A wonderful bird is a pelican. His bill will hold more than his belican!" • Single birds seen in winter are often sick or injured.

Other ID: *Breeding:* small, keeled plate develops on upper mandible; pale yellow crest on back of head. *Nonbreeding* and *immature:* white plumage is tinged with brown; short tail.
Size: L 4½–6 ft; W 9 ft.
Voice: generally quiet; rarely issues piglike grunts.
Status: common or locally abundant migrant; rare in summer and winter.
Habitat: lakes; river mouths and marshes.

Similar Birds

Snow Goose
(p. 20)

Look For

When pelicans fly into the wind, they often stay close to the surface of the water. When they have a tailwind, they will fly much higher.

American White Pelican 49

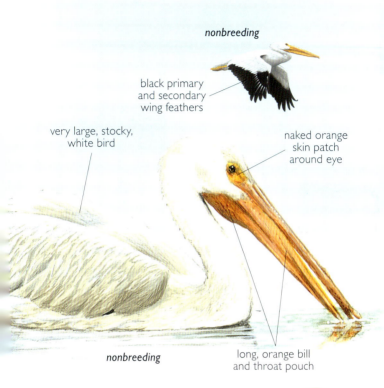

nonbreeding

black primary and secondary wing feathers

very large, stocky, white bird

naked orange skin patch around eye

nonbreeding

long, orange bill and throat pouch

Nesting: does not nest in Oklahoma; breeds on lakes throughout the northern Great Plains and mountainous West; colonial; on a bare, low-lying island; nest scrape is unlined or lined with twigs; dull white eggs are 3⅜ x 2¼ in; pair incubates 2 eggs for 29–36 days.

Did You Know?

The feathers on a pelican's wing tips are black and have a pigment called melanin that doesn't wear away in the wind. All other large, white birds with black wing tips fly with their necks extended; the American White Pelican is the only one to fly with its neck pulled back towards its wings.

Double-crested Cormorant
Phalacrocorax auritus

The Double-crested Cormorant looks like a bird but swims and smells like a fish. With a long, rudderlike tail and excellent underwater vision, this slick-feathered bird has mastered the underwater world. Most water birds have waterproof feathers, but the structure of the Double-crested Cormorant's feathers allow water in. "Wettable" feathers make this bird less buoyant, which in turn makes it a better diver. The Double-crested Cormorant also has sealed nostrils for diving, and therefore must fly with its bill open. • A close relative, the Neotropic Cormorant, is a rare visitor to Oklahoma, usually in the summer.

Other ID: all-black body; blue eyes. *Nonbreeding:* no plumes trail from eyebrows. *Immature:* brown upperparts; buff throat and breast; yellowish throat patch. *In flight:* rapid wingbeats; kinked neck.
Size: *L* 26–32 in; *W* 4¼ ft.
Voice: generally quiet.
Status: common to abundant migrant; uncommon in winter and summer; rare local nesting species.
Habitat: large lakes and large rivers.

Similar Birds

Common Loon

Neotropic Cormorant

Anhinga

Double-crested Cormorant

- fine, black plumes trail from eyebrows
- thin bill, hooked at tip
- orange-yellow throat pouch
- long, crooked neck
- *juvenile*
- *Eastern Form; breeding*

Nesting: colonial; on an island or high in a tree; platform nest is made of sticks and guano; pale blue eggs are 2 x 1½ in; both sexes incubate 2–7 eggs for 25–30 days.

Did You Know?

Japanese fishermen sometimes use cormorants on leashes to catch fish. This traditional method of fishing is called *Ukai*.

Look For

Double-crested Cormorants often perch on trees or piers with their wings partially spread. Lacking oil glands, they use the wind to dry their feathers.

Great Blue Heron
Ardea herodias

The Great Blue Heron is one of the best-known wading birds in Oklahoma. • They are often mistakenly called cranes, but unlike cranes, which hold their necks outstretched in flight, herons fly with their long necks tucked toward their bodies. • Great Blue Herons nest in colonies known as rookeries, which can contain dozens to thousands of pairs and usually include other species of water birds. Rookeries are usually located on isolated islands or in wooded swamps to avoid terrestrial predators such as raccoons. Nesting herons are sensitive to human disturbance, so observe this bird's behavior from a distance.

Other ID: large, blue-gray wading bird; long, dark legs; blue-gray back and wing coverts. *Breeding:* richer colors; plumes on crown and throat. *In flight:* slow, steady wingbeats.
Size: *L* 4–4½ ft; *W* 6 ft.
Voice: deep *frahnk-frahnk-frahnk* when startled.
Status: common summer resident; uncommon in winter near open water.
Habitat: forages along the edges of wetlands; also stalks fields or yards.

Similar Birds

Sandhill Crane

Tricolored Heron

Little Blue Heron

Great Blue Heron 53

- neck folds back over shoulders
- black plumes above eye
- large, straight yellow bill
- long, curving neck with black markings on throat
- chestnut brown thighs

breeding

Nesting: colonial; stick platform up to 4 ft in diameter is built in a tree or shrub; pale greenish blue eggs are 2½ x 1¾ in; pair incubates 3–5 eggs for 22–24 days.

Did You Know?

Although Great Blue Herons mostly feed on fish and other aquatic life, sometimes they can be seen feeding on rodents in fields and meadows.

Look For

Great Blue Herons typically are solitary feeders, whereas Sandhill Cranes are usually seen feeding in groups.

Great Egret
Ardea alba

The plumes of the Great Egret and Snowy Egret were widely used to decorate women's hats during the early 20th century. An ounce of egret feathers cost as much as $32—more than an ounce of gold at the time! The outcry over the killing of egrets for the sake of fashion eventually led to some of the most successful conservation legislation in North America. Today Great Egrets are again abundant and breed farther north than they did historically. • Egrets are named after their silky breeding plumes, called aigrettes, which most species grow during courtship. The aigrettes of a Great Egret can reach up to 4½ feet long!

Other ID: large, all-white wading bird; green skin patch between eyes and base of bill; long plumes. *In flight:* slow wingbeats; neck folds back over shoulders; legs extend backward.
Size: *L* 3–3½ ft; *W* 4 ft.
Voice: generally silent away from colonies.
Status: common migrant; locally common summer resident.
Habitat: edges of marshes, lakes and ponds; flooded agricultural fields.

Similar Birds

Snowy Egret

Cattle Egret

Little Blue Heron (immature)

Great Egret

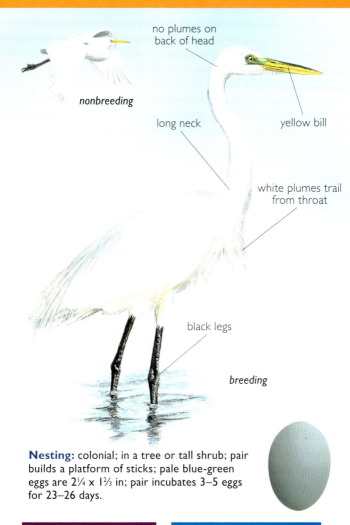

nonbreeding

- no plumes on back of head
- long neck
- yellow bill
- white plumes trail from throat
- black legs

breeding

Nesting: colonial; in a tree or tall shrub; pair builds a platform of sticks; pale blue-green eggs are 2¼ x 1⅔ in; pair incubates 3–5 eggs for 23–26 days.

Did You Know?

The Great Egret is the symbol of the National Audubon Society, one of our nation's oldest conservation organizations.

Look For

Because of their long legs and long neck, Great Egrets can forage in deeper water than other egrets.

Black-crowned Night-Heron

Nycticorax nycticorax

When dusk's long shadows shroud the marshes, the Black-crowned Night-Herons arrive to hunt in the marshy waters. These herons crouch motionless, using their large, light-sensitive eyes to spot prey lurking in the shallows. • The Black-crowned Night-Heron breeds throughout much of the United States and is the most abundant heron in the world. Watch for them in summer, between dawn and dusk, as they fly from nesting colonies to feeding areas and back. • Another night-heron common in Oklahoma is the Yellow-crowned Night-Heron.

Other ID: black back; gray neck and wings; dull yellow legs; stout, black bill.
Size: *L* 23–26 in; *W* 3½ ft.
Voice: deep, guttural *quark* or *wok*, often heard as the bird takes flight.
Status: uncommon migrant; widely scattered nesting species.
Habitat: shallow cattail and bulrush marshes, lakeshores and along slow-flowing rivers.

Similar Birds

Yellow-crowned Night-Heron

Green Heron

American Bittern

Black-crowned Night-Heron 57

- feet protrude only slightly beyond tail
- *immature*
- black cap with 2 white plumes
- large, red eyes
- white cheek
- *breeding*
- stocky body

Nesting: colonial; in a tree or shrub; male gathers nest material; female builds a loose nest platform of twigs and sticks and lines it with finer materials; pale green eggs are 2¼ x 1 in; pair incubates 3–4 eggs for 21–26 days.

Did You Know?

Nycticorax, meaning "night raven," refers to this bird's distinctive nighttime calls.

Look For

A heron can sometimes be seen swimming, looking like a strange duck.

58 Herons & Vultures

Turkey Vulture
Cathartes aura

Turkey Vultures are intelligent, playful and social birds. Groups live and sleep together in large trees, or "roosts." Some roost sites are over a century old and have been used by the same family of vultures for several generations. • The genus name *Cathartes* means "cleanser" and refers to this bird's affinity for carrion. A vulture's bill and feet are much less powerful than those of eagles, hawks or falcons, which kill live prey. Its red, featherless head may appear grotesque, but this adaptation allows the bird to stay relatively clean while feeding on messy carcasses. • Vultures appear small headed compared to eagles, which have feathered heads.

Other ID: *Immature:* gray head. *In flight:* head appears small; rocks from side to side when soaring.
Size: *L* 25–31 in; *W* 5½–6 ft.
Voice: generally silent; occasionally produces a hiss or grunt if threatened.
Status: common migrant and summer resident; uncommon winter resident in the southeast.
Habitat: usually flies over open country, shorelines or roads, rarely over forests.

Similar Birds

Golden Eagle

Bald Eagle
(p. 62)

Black Vulture

Turkey Vulture 59

- wings are held in a shallow "V"
- silver gray flight feathers
- bare, red head
- pale, hooked bill
- brownish overall

Nesting: in a cave, crevice, log or among boulders; uses no nest material; darkly marked, dull white eggs are 2¾ x 2 in; pair incubates 2–3 eggs for up to 41 days.

Did You Know?

A threatened Turkey Vulture will play dead or throw up. The odor of its vomit repulses attackers, much like the odor of a skunk's spray.

Look For

No other Oklahoma bird uses updrafts and thermals in flight as well as the Turkey Vulture. Pilots have reported seeing vultures soaring at 20,000 feet.

Mississippi Kite
Ictinia mississippiensis

Most often seen in flight, the Mississippi Kite floats buoyantly above the southern plains, flapping lazily but rarely gliding. This bird feeds on flying insects such as dragonflies, cicadas, beetles and grasshoppers, which are plucked out of the air with the bird's feet and eaten while in flight. Occasional, acrobatic aerial pursuits end in the successful capture of vertebrates, including bats, swallows and swifts. • Mississippi Kites were traditionally restricted to the southern states, but their breeding range is expanding northward, as far as southern New England.

Other ID: chestnut at base of primaries is often inconspicuous. *In flight:* gray overall; male has white inner wing patches; short outermost primary feather. *Juvenile:* dark brownish upperparts; underparts heavily marked with rufous; banded tail.
Size: *L* 14 in; *W* 3 ft.
Voice: generally silent; alarm call is *kee-kew, kew-kew;* call of fledgling an emphatic *three-beers.*
Status: common summer resident, except rare in northwest.
Habitat: deciduous or mixed woodlands, riparian areas, shelterbelts and towns.

Similar Birds

Peregrine Falcon

Sharp-shinned Hawk

Cooper's Hawk (p. 66)

Mississippi Kite 61

Nesting: in a tall tree; pair constructs a flimsy stick platform lined with leaves; bluish white eggs are 1⅝ x 1⅜ in; pair incubates 2 eggs for 30–32 days.

Did You Know?

Kites disperse northward after the breeding season and flocks can be seen returning south in early fall.

Look For

Sometimes kites show aggressive behavior toward humans and pets around nest sites in residential areas.

Bald Eagle
Haliaeetus leucocephalus

While soaring hundreds of feet in the air, a Bald Eagle can spot fish swimming underwater or small rodents scurrying through the grass. This majestic bird also scavenges carrion and steals food from other birds. • Eagles, Turkey Vultures and Ospreys can be told apart when they are in flight. The wings of eagles are held flat as they soar, Turkey Vultures hold their wings tilted up in a "V," and the wings of Ospreys appear to be droop below the horizontal. • In 1990, no Bald Eagles nested in Oklahoma, but today more than 30 pairs nest in our state.

Other ID: *1st year:* dark overall; dark bill; some white in underwings. *2nd year:* dark "bib"; white in underwings. *3rd year:* mostly white plumage; yellow at base of bill; yellow eyes. *4th year:* light head with dark facial streak; variable pale and dark plumage; yellow bill; paler eyes.
Size: *L* 30–43 in; *W* 5½–8 ft.
Voice: thin, weak squeal or gull-like cackle: *kleek-kik-kik-kik* or *kah-kah-kah*.
Status: common winter resident near large reservoirs; uncommon nesting species.
Habitat: near large lakes and rivers.

Similar Birds

Golden Eagle

Osprey

Bald Eagle 63

Nesting: usually in a tree bordering a lake or large river; huge stick nest is often reused for many years; white eggs are 2¾ x 2⅛ in; pair incubates 1–3 eggs for 34–36 days.

Did You Know?

In winter, hundreds of ducks and geese gather on reservoirs or other ice-free waters in Oklahoma, providing an easy meal for hungry Bald Eagles.

Look For

Bald Eagles do not mature until their fourth or fifth year—only then do they develop the characteristic white head and tail plumage.

Northern Harrier
Circus cyaneus

With its prominent white rump and distinctive slightly upturned wings, the Northern Harrier may be the easiest raptor to identify in flight. Unlike other midsized birds, it often flies close to the ground, relying on sudden surprise attacks to capture prey. • The courtship flight of the Northern Harrier is a spectacle worth watching in spring. The male climbs almost vertically in the air, then stalls and plummets in a reckless dive toward the ground. At the last second he saves himself with a hairpin turn that sends him skyward again.

Other ID: *Male:* bluish gray to silver gray upperparts; white underparts; indistinct tail bands, except for 1 dark subterminal band. *Female:* dark brown upperparts; streaky, brown and buff underparts. *In flight:* long wings and tail; black wing tips.
Size: *L* 16–24 in; *W* 3½–4 ft.
Voice: generally quiet; high-pitched *ke-ke-ke-ke-ke-ke* near the nest or during courtship.
Status: common migrant and winter resident; uncommon summer resident.
Habitat: open country, including fields, wet meadows, cattail marshes and croplands.

Similar Birds

Rough-legged Hawk

Ferruginous Hawk

Northern Harrier

white rump

facial disc

yellow legs

long, dark-banded tail

Nesting: on the ground; usually in tall vegetation or on a raised mound; shallow depression is lined with grass, sticks and cattails; bluish white eggs are 1⅞ x 1⅜ in; female incubates 4–6 eggs for 30–32 days.

Did You Know?

Britain's Royal Air Force was so impressed by the Northern Harrier's maneuverability that it named the Harrier aircraft after this bird.

Look For

The Northern Harrier's owl-like, parabolic facial disc enhances its hearing, allowing this bird to hunt by sound as well as sight.

Cooper's Hawk
Accipiter cooperii

immature

Cooper's Hawk will quickly change the scene at a backyard bird feeder when it comes looking for a meal. European Starlings, American Robins and House Sparrows are among its favorite choices of prey. • You might also spot this songbird scavenger hunting along forest edges. With the help of its long tail, short, rounded wings and flap-and-glide flight, it is capable of maneuvering quickly at high speeds to snatch its prey in midair.

Other ID: short, rounded wings; dark barring on pale undertail and underwings; blue-gray back; white terminal tail band.
Size: *Male:* L 15–17 in; W 27–32 in.
Female: L 17–19 in; W 32–37 in.
Voice: fast, woodpecker-like *cac-cac-cac-cac*.
Status: uncommon migrant and winter resident; widely scattered in summer.
Habitat: mixed woodlands, riparian woodlands, urban gardens with feeders.

Similar Birds

Sharp-shinned Hawk

Northern Goshawk

Broad-winged Hawk

Cooper's Hawk

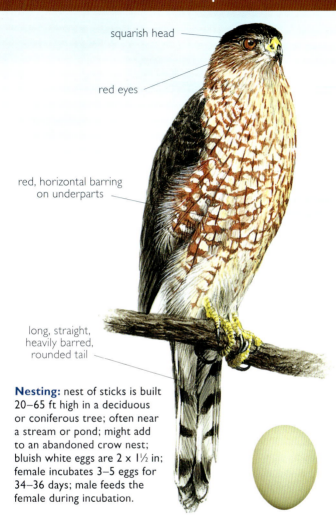

- squarish head
- red eyes
- red, horizontal barring on underparts
- long, straight, heavily barred, rounded tail

Nesting: nest of sticks is built 20–65 ft high in a deciduous or coniferous tree; often near a stream or pond; might add to an abandoned crow nest; bluish white eggs are 2 x 1½ in; female incubates 3–5 eggs for 34–36 days; male feeds the female during incubation.

Did You Know?

Female birds of prey are always larger than the males. The female Cooper's Hawk does not hesitate to hunt birds as large as a Rock Pigeon.

Look For

Cooper's Hawks have been known to run after prey on the ground for short distances.

Swainson's Hawk
Buteo swainsoni

The Swainson's Hawk dominates the skies in the open, grassy expanses of Oklahoma where small rodents are abundant. It is also attracted to prairie fires. • Twice a year, Swainson's Hawks undertake long migratory journeys that may lead them as far south as the southern tip of South America and as far north as Alaska. Traveling up to 12,500 miles a year, it is second only to the Peregrine Falcon for long-distance travel among birds of prey. It is occasionally seen in large flocks in Oklahoma, especially in late September.

Other ID: *Dark morph:* dark overall; brown wing linings blend with flight feathers. *Light morph:* white wing linings contrast with dark flight feathers. *In flight:* long wings with pointed tips; holds wings in shallow "V."
Size: *L* 19–22 in; *W* 4½ ft.
Voice: typical hawk call, *keeeaar,* is higher pitched than a Red-tailed Hawk's.
Status: common summer resident in the west; rare in eastern Oklahoma; sometimes abundant during migration.
Habitat: open fields, grasslands, sagebrush and agricultural areas.

Similar Birds

Red-tailed Hawk (p. 70)

Red-shouldered Hawk

Broad-winged Hawk

Swainson's Hawk 69

- dark edges on outerwings
- narrowly banded tail
- light morph
- white face
- dark "bib"
- white belly

Nesting: nests in a tree or shrub adjacent to open habitat; stick nest is lined with bark and fresh leaves; brown-spotted, whitish eggs are 2¼ x 1¾ in; pair incubates 2–4 eggs for 28–35 days.

Did You Know?

The "kettles" of Swainson's Hawks migrating have been likened to the legendary flocks of Passenger Pigeons that were said to blacken the sky.

Look For

Pointed wing tips, slightly upturned wings and dark flight feathers differentiate the Swainson's Hawk from all other raptors in flight.

Red-tailed Hawk
Buteo jamaicensis

Take an afternoon drive through the country and look for Red-tailed Hawks soaring above the fields. Red-tails are the most common hawks in Oklahoma, especially in winter. • In warm weather, these hawks use thermals and updrafts to soar. The pockets of rising air provide substantial lift, which allows migrating hawks to fly for almost 2 miles without flapping their wings. On cooler days, resident Red-tails perch on exposed tree limbs, fence posts or utility poles to scan for prey. • The Harlan's Hawk, a dark race of the Red-tailed Hawk, is a winter visitor to Oklahoma.

Other ID: brown eyes; overall color varies geographically. *In flight:* light underwing flight feathers with faint barring; dark leading edge on underside of wings. *Juvenile:* dark shoulder patches.
Size: *Male:* L 18–23 in; W 4–5 ft. *Female:* L 20–25 in; W 4–5 ft.
Voice: powerful, descending scream, *keeearrrr.*
Status: common year-round resident.
Habitat: open country with some trees; also roadsides, woodlots and urban areas.

Similar Birds

Rough-legged Hawk

Red-shouldered Hawk

Swainson's Hawk (p. 68)

Red-tailed Hawk 71

- dark upperparts with some white highlights
- Harlan's Hawk
- white, fan-shaped tail
- dark leading edge
- dark brown band of streaks across belly
- red tail

Nesting: in woodlands adjacent to open habitat; bulky stick nest is enlarged each year; brown-blotched, whitish eggs are 2⅜ x 1⅞ in; pair incubates 2–4 eggs for 28–35 days.

Did You Know?

The Red-tailed Hawk's piercing call is often paired with the image of an eagle in TV commercials and movies.

Look For

Courting pairs will dive at each other, lock talons and tumble toward the earth. They break away at the last second to avoid crashing into the ground.

American Kestrel
Falco sparverius

The colorful American Kestrel, formerly known as the "Sparrow Hawk," is a common and widespread falcon, not shy of human activity and adaptable to habitat change. This small falcon has benefited from the grassy medians created by interstate highways, which provide habitat for grasshoppers and other small prey. Watch for this robin-sized bird along rural roadways, perched on poles and telephone wires or hovering over fields as it forages for food. It is also found in cities, where it uses industrial areas, vacant lots, landfills and highway interchanges for hunting rodents, large insects and even House Sparrows.

Other ID: *In flight:* frequently hovers; buoyant, indirect flight style. *Male:* blue-gray crown with rusty cap.
Size: *L* 7½–8 in; *W* 20–24 in.
Voice: usually silent; loud, often repeated, shrill *killy-killy-killy* when excited; female's voice is lower pitched.
Status: common resident throughout most of the state, but uncommon in southeast.
Habitat: open fields, riparian woodlands, woodlots, forest edges, roadside ditches, grasslands and croplands.

Similar Birds

Merlin

Prairie Falcon

Sharp-shinned Hawk

American Kestrel

Nesting: in a tree cavity; may use a nest box; white to pale brown, speckled eggs are 1½ x 1⅛ in; mostly the female incubates 4–6 eggs for 29–30 days; both adults raise the young.

Did You Know?
No stranger to captivity, the American Kestrel has been used extensively to study the effects of pesticides on birds of prey.

Look For
The American Kestrel repeatedly lifts its tail while perched.

American Coot
Fulica americana

Though they resemble ducks, American Coots are actually more closely related to rails and gallinules. Many features distinguish a coot from a duck, including head-bobbing while swimming or walking, a narrower bill that extends up the forehead and the lack of fully webbed feet. • Coots squabble constantly during the breeding season and can often be seen running along the surface of the water, splashing and charging at intruders. Outside of the breeding season, coots gather in large, amicable groups. During spring and fall, thousands congregate at a few staging areas in Oklahoma.

Other ID: red eyes; long, yellow-green legs; lobed toes; small, white marks on tail.
Size: *L* 13–16 in; *W* 24 in.
Voice: calls frequently in summer, day and night: *kuk-kuk-kuk-kuk-kuk;* also croaks and grunts.
Status: common to abundant migrant and winter resident; rare summer resident.
Habitat: shallow marshes, ponds and wetlands with open water and emergent vegetation; also sewage lagoons.

Similar Birds

Common Moorhen

Sora

American Coot 75

reddish spot on white forehead shield

white, chicken-like bill with dark ring around tip

Nesting: in emergent vegetation; pair builds a floating nest of cattails and grass; buffy white, brown-spotted eggs are 2 x 1⅜ in; pair incubates 8–12 eggs for 21–25 days; may raise 2 broods.

Did You Know?

American Coots, sometimes called "Mudhens," are the most widespread and abundant rails in North America.

Look For

With a narrow bill, a bobbing head and feet that have individually webbed toes, a coot looks somewhat like a cross between a chicken and a duck.

Killdeer
Charadrius vociferus

The Killdeer is a gifted actor, well known for its "broken wing" distraction display. When an intruder wanders too close to its nest, the Killdeer greets the interloper with piteous cries while dragging a wing and stumbling about as if injured. Most predators take the bait and follow, and once the Killdeer has lured the predator far away from its nest, it miraculously recovers from the injury and flies off with a loud call. • The Killdeer is one of the first birds to return in spring, sometimes returning too soon and becoming a casualty of early-spring snow and ice storms.

Other ID: brown head; white neck band; brown back and upperwings; white underparts; rufous rump. *Immature:* downy; only 1 breast band.
Size: *L* 9–11 in; *W* 24 in.
Voice: loud, distinctive *kill-dee kill-dee kill-deer;* variations include *deer-deer.*
Status: common summer resident; uncommon in winter.
Habitat: open areas, such as fields, lakeshores, sandy beaches, mudflats, gravel streambeds, wet meadows and grasslands.

Similar Birds

Semipalmated Plover

Piping Plover

Snowy Plover

Killdeer 77

- white eyebrow and patch above bill
- black forehead band
- 2 black breast bands
- long, pinkish legs

Nesting: on open ground, in a shallow, usually unlined depression; heavily marked, creamy buff eggs are 1 3/8 x 1 1/8 in; pair incubates 4 eggs for 24–28 days; may raise 2 broods.

Did You Know?
You might hear a European Starling imitate the Killdeer's call.

Look For
The Killdeer has adapted well to urbanization, and it finds golf courses, farms, fields and abandoned industrial areas much to its liking.

Spotted Sandpiper
Actitis macularius

The female Spotted Sandpiper, unlike most other female birds, lays her eggs and leaves the male to tend the clutch. She diligently defends her territory and may mate with several different males. Of the world's bird species, only about one percent display this unusual breeding strategy known as "polyandry." Each summer, the female can lay up to four clutches and is capable of producing 20 eggs. As the season progresses, however, available males become harder to find; come August, there may be seven females for every available male.

Other ID: *Nonbreeding* and *immature:* pure white breast, foreneck and throat; brown bill; dull yellow legs. *In flight:* flies close to the water's surface with very rapid, shallow, stiff-winged strokes.
Size: *L* 7–8 in; *W* 15 in.
Voice: sharp, crisp *eat-wheat, eat-wheat, wheat-wheat-wheat-wheat*.
Status: common migrant; rare nesting species.
Habitat: shorelines, gravel beaches, drainage ditches, swamps and sewage lagoons; occasionally seen in cultivated fields.

Similar Birds

Solitary Sandpiper

Dunlin

Sanderling

Spotted Sandpiper 79

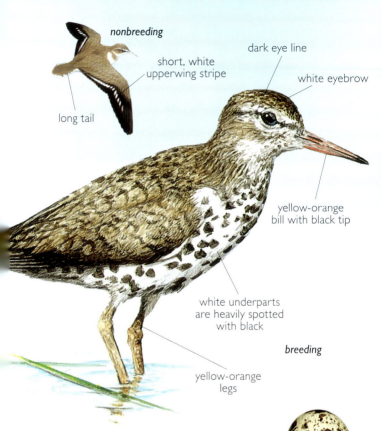

nonbreeding — short, white upperwing stripe — long tail

dark eye line — white eyebrow — yellow-orange bill with black tip — white underparts are heavily spotted with black — *breeding* — yellow-orange legs

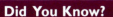

Nesting: usually near water; shallow scrape is lined with grass and sheltered by vegetation; darkly blotched, creamy buff eggs are 1¼ x 1 in; male incubates 4 eggs for 20–24 days.

Did You Know?

Sandpipers have four toes: three pointing forward and one pointing backward. Plovers, such as the Killdeer, have only three toes.

Look For

Spotted Sandpipers bob their tails constantly on shore and fly with rapid, shallow, stiff-winged strokes.

Lesser Yellowlegs
Tringa flavipes

The "tattletale" Lesser Yellowlegs is the self-appointed sentinel in a mixed flock of shorebirds, raising the alarm at the first sign of a threat. • It is challenging to discern the Lesser Yellowlegs from the Greater Yellowlegs *(T. melanoleuca)* in the field, but with practice, you will notice that the Lesser's bill is finer, straighter and shorter, about as long as its head is wide. The Lesser is also more commonly seen in flocks. Finally, the Lesser Yellowlegs emits a pair of peeps, while the Greater Yellowlegs peeps three times.
• In Oklahoma, fall migration for shorebirds begins in late July. Spring migration is mostly in April and May.

Other ID: subtle, dark eye line; pale lores. *Nonbreeding:* grayer overall.
Size: *L* 10–11 in; *W* 24 in.
Voice: typically a high-pitched pair of *tew* notes; noisiest on breeding grounds.
Status: common migrant.
Habitat: shorelines of lakes, rivers, marshes and ponds.

Similar Birds

Willet

Greater Yellowlegs

Solitary Sandpiper

Lesser Yellowlegs 81

nonbreeding

brown-black mottling on upperparts

all-dark bill is not noticeably longer than width of head

bright yellow legs

lacks barring on belly

breeding

Nesting: does not nest in Oklahoma; nests in the Arctic; in a natural forest opening; in a depression on a dry mound lined with leaves and grass; darkly blotched, buff to olive eggs are 1⅝ x 1⅛ in; pair incubates 4 eggs for 22–23 days.

Did You Know?

Yellowlegs were popular game birds in the 1800s because they were plentiful and easy to shoot.

Look For

When feeding, the Lesser Yellowlegs wades into water almost to its belly, sweeping its bill back and forth just below the water's surface.

Baird's Sandpiper
Calidris bairdii

Migrating farther and faster than most birds, Baird's Sandpipers complete their 9300 mile journey from the high Arctic to the tip of South America in just five weeks. The adults leave their northern breeding grounds soon after the chicks hatch and are able to fend for themselves, migrating to the staging areas in the Canadian Prairies and northern Great Plains. There they refuel on insects for what is often a direct, nonstop journey to South America. Once the young accumulate fat reserves, they follow in a second wave of southbound migrants.

Other ID: *Nonbreeding:* folded wings extend beyond tail. *Breeding:* large, black, diamondlike pattern on back and wing coverts.
Size: *L* 7–7½ in; *W* 17 in.
Voice: soft, rolling *kriit kriit*.
Status: common migrant.
Habitat: sandy beaches, wet fields, mudflats and wetland edges.

Similar Birds

Semipalmated Sandpiper

Pectoral Sandpiper

Least Sandpiper

Baird's Sandpiper 83

distinctive, "scaly" back

black bill

faint, buff brown breast speckling

nonbreeding

black legs

Nesting: does not nest in Oklahoma; nests in the Arctic; on dry, sparsely vegetated tundra; in a shallow depression lined with grass; buff eggs, blotched with reddish-brown are 1 3/8 x 1 in; both adults incubate 4 eggs for 21 days.

Did You Know?

The Baird's Sandpiper invests more in egg production than most birds. The female lays four eggs that may total up to 120 percent of her body mass.

Look For

This sandpiper belongs to a group of shorebirds called "peeps," which include the Least, Semipalmated, Western and White-rumped sandpipers.

Franklin's Gull
Larus pipixcan

The Franklin's Gull is not a typical "sea gull." This land-loving bird spends much of its life inland and nests on the prairies, where it is affectionately known as "Prairie Dove." It often follows tractors across agricultural fields, snatching up insects from the tractor's path in much the same way its cousins follow fishing boats. • Franklin's Gull is one of only a few gull species that migrate long distances between breeding and wintering grounds—the majority of Franklin's Gulls overwinter along the Pacific coast of Peru and Chile.

Other ID: *Nonbreeding:* incomplete, white eye ring; dark patch on back of whitish head; black legs.
Size: *L* 13–15 in; *W* 3 ft.
Voice: shrill, "mewing" *weeeh-ah weeeh-ah* while feeding and in migration; also a shrill *kuk-kuk-kuk*.
Status: abundant migrant; rare in summer and winter.
Habitat: agricultural fields, marshy lakes, landfills and large river and lake shorelines.

Similar Birds

Bonaparte's Gull   Laughing Gull   Caspian Tern

Franklin's Gull 85

Nesting: does not nest in Oklahoma; nests in the Canadian prairies and northern Great Plains; colonial; usually in dense emergent vegetation; floating platform nest is built above water; variably marked, pale greenish or buff eggs are 2 x 1⅜ in; pair incubates 3 eggs for 25 days.

Did You Know?

This gull was named for Sir John Franklin, the British explorer who led four expeditions to the Canadian Arctic in the 19th century.

Look For

Tens of thousands of Franklin's Gulls linger on large reservoirs during fall migration. In spring, smaller flocks move through to the breeding grounds more quickly.

Ring-billed Gull
Larus delawarensis

Few people can claim that they have never seen this common and widespread gull. Highly tolerant of humans, Ring-billed Gulls are part of our everyday lives, scavenging our litter and frequenting our parks. These omnivorous gulls will eat almost anything and will swarm parks, beaches, golf courses and fast-food parking lots looking for food handouts, making pests of themselves. However, few species have adjusted to human development as well as the Ring-billed Gull, which is something to appreciate.

Other ID: *Breeding:* white head and upperparts. *In flight:* pale gray mantle.
Size: *L* 18–20 in; *W* 4 ft.
Voice: high-pitched *kakakaka-akakaka;* also a low, laughlike *yook-yook-yook*.
Status: common migrant and winter resident.
Habitat: *Breeding:* bare, rocky and shrubby islands and sewage ponds. *In migration* and *winter:* lakes, rivers, landfills, golf courses, large parking lots, fields and parks.

Similar Birds

Herring Gull   Glaucous Gull

Ring-billed Gull 87

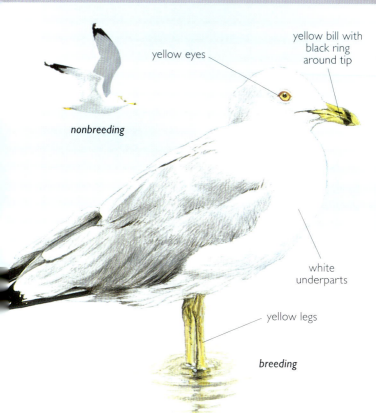

nonbreeding

yellow eyes

yellow bill with black ring around tip

white underparts

yellow legs

breeding

Nesting: does not nest in Oklahoma; nests in northern U.S. and Canada; colonial; in a shallow scrape on the ground, lined with grass, debris and small sticks; brown-blotched, gray to olive eggs are 2⅜ x 1⅝ in; pair incubates 2–4 eggs for 23–28 days.

Did You Know?

In chaotic nesting colonies, adult Ring-billed Gulls will call out and recognize the response of their chicks.

Look For

To differentiate between gulls, pay attention to the markings on their bills and the color of their legs and eyes.

Forster's Tern
Sterna forsteri

The Forster's Tern so closely resembles the Common Tern *(S. hirundo)* that the two often seem indistinguishable. Look closely and you will notice that the bill of the Common is darker red whereas the Forster's bill is orange. • Forster's Tern has an exclusively North American breeding distribution, but it bears the name of a man who never visited this continent: German naturalist Johann Reinhold Forster (1729–98). Forster, who lived and worked in England, examined tern specimens sent from Hudson Bay, Canada. He was the first to recognize this bird as a distinct species.

Other ID: light gray mantle; white rump; long, gray tail with white outer edges. *Breeding:* black cap and nape; large, orange black-tipped bill. *In flight:* forked, gray tail; long, pointed wings.
Size: L 14–16 in; W 31 in.
Voice: flight call is a nasal, short *keer keer*; also a grating *tzaap*.
Status: uncommon migrant; rare in summer and winter.
Habitat: coastal areas; brackish wetlands; freshwater lakes, rivers and marshes.

Similar Birds

Common Tern   Least Tern   Black Tern

Forster's Tern 89

nonbreeding

black band through eyes

black bill

pure white underparts

orange legs

breeding

Nesting: does not nest in Oklahoma; nests locally throughout North America; occasionally colonial; nest is a platform of floating vegetation in freshwater or saltwater marshes; olive to buff, blotched eggs are 1 5/8 x 1 1/4 in; pair incubates 2–3 eggs for 24 days.

Did You Know?

The bill color of the Forster's Tern changes from black in winter to orange with a black tip in summer.

Look For

Like most terns, the Forster's Tern catches fish in dramatic headfirst dives, but it also snatches flying insects in mid-air with graceful swoops, twists and turns.

Rock Pigeon
Columba livia

Rock Pigeons are familiar to just about anyone who has lived in the city. These colorful, acrobatic, seed-eating birds frequent parks, town squares, railroad yards and factory sites. Their tolerance of humans has made them a source of entertainment, as well as a pest. • This pigeon is likely a descendant of a Eurasian bird that was first domesticated about 4500 BC. Settlers introduced the Rock Pigeon to North America in the 17th century. "Homing Pigeons" carried strategic messages during World War II and saved hundreds of lives.

Other ID: usually has white rump and orange feet.
In flight: holds wings in a deep "V" while gliding.
Size: L 12–13 in; W 28 in (male is usually larger).
Voice: soft, cooing *coorrr-coorrr-coorrr.*
Status: common permanent resident.
Habitat: urban areas, railroad yards and agricultural areas.

Similar Birds

Eurasian Collared-Dove (p. 92)

Look For

No other "wild" bird varies as much in coloration, a result of semi-domestication and extensive inbreeding over time.

Rock Pigeon 91

color is highly variable (iridescent blue-gray, red, white or tan)

white cere

Nesting: in a barn or on a cliff, bridge or tower; in a flimsy nest of sticks, grass and other vegetation; glossy white eggs are 1½ x 1⅛ in; pair incubates 2 eggs for 16–19 days; may raise broods year-round.

Did You Know?

These birds are some of the most well-studied birds in the world. Much of our understanding of bird migration, endocrinology, color genetics and sensory perception comes from experiments involving Rock Pigeons.

Eurasian Collared-Dove
Streptopelia decaocto

About 50 Eurasian Collared-Doves were released in the Bahamas in 1974 and probably reached the southeastern Florida peninsula that same decade, but because they so closely resemble the domestic Ringed Turtle-Dove, they were overlooked. They were finally "discovered" on the North American mainland in 1986. Eurasian Collared-Doves have now spread across much of the continent. They were first discovered in Oklahoma in 1996 and the first nest was found in 1996. Colonization of Central and South America can also be expected.
• *Streptopelia* is Greek for "twisted dove."

Other ID: a large chunky dove; square tail with white outer tail feathers.
Size: *L* 12–13 in; *W* 18–20 in.
Voice: a low *coo-COO-coo,* repeated incessantly throughout the day.
Status: increasing and spreading, especially in rural areas.
Habitat: primarily associated with humans; urban and suburban areas.

Similar Birds

Mourning Dove (p. 94)

White-winged Dove

Eurasian Collared-Dove 93

- black hind-collar is outlined in white
- pale gray overall
- dark wing tips

Nesting: in a tree; female builds a platform of twigs and sticks; white eggs are 1¼ x ⅞ in; pair incubates 2 eggs for about 14 days; may raise 3 or more broods in a season.

Did You Know?

Native to India and southeast Asia, these doves dramatically expanded into other parts of Asia, Europe and Africa during the 20th century.

Look For

These doves feed on grain and are frequently seen near grain elevators and at bird feeders.

Mourning Dove
Zenaida macroura

The Mourning Dove's soft cooing, which filters through broken woodlands and suburban parks, is often confused with the sound of a hooting owl. Beginning birders who track down the source of the calls are often surprised to find the streamlined silhouette of a perched dove. • This popular game animal is common throughout Oklahoma and is one of the most abundant native birds in North America. Human development has proven beneficial to this species by providing more open habitats and a variety of new food sources.

Other ID: buffy, gray-brown plumage; small head; dark bill; sleek body; dull red legs.
Size: *L* 11–13 in; *W* 18 in.
Voice: mournful, soft, slow *oh-woe-woe-woe*.
Status: common summer resident and migrant; less common in winter.
Habitat: open and riparian woodlands, forest edges, agricultural and suburban areas, open parks.

Similar Birds

Yellow-billed Cuckoo (p. 96)

White-winged Dove

Mourning Dove 95

- pale blue eye ring
- dark, shiny patch below ear
- pale rosy underparts
- black spots on upperwing
- long, white-trimmed, tapering tail

Nesting: in a shrub or tree; occasionally on the ground; nest is a fragile, shallow platform of twigs; white eggs are 1⅛ x ⅞ in; pair incubates 2 eggs for 14 days.

Did You Know?

The Mourning Dove raises up to six broods each year—more than any other native bird.

Look For

When the Mourning Dove bursts into flight, its wings clap above and below its body. It also often creates a whistling sound as it flies at high speed.

Yellow-billed Cuckoo
Coccyzus americanus

Tracts of forest with plenty of clearings and even large shelterbelts provide valuable habitat for the Yellow-billed Cuckoo, a bird that is declining over much of its range and has already disappeared in some states. The cuckoo's habitat is also steadily disappearing as waterways are altered or dammed.
• The cuckoo skillfully negotiates its tangled home within impenetrable, deciduous undergrowth in silence, relying on obscurity for survival. Then, for a short period during nesting, the male cuckoo tempts fate by issuing a barrage of loud, rhythmic courtship calls.

Other ID: olive brown upperparts; white underparts.
Size: *L* 11–13 in; *W* 18 in.
Voice: long series of deep, hollow *kuks*, slowing near the end: *kuk-kuk-kuk-kuk kuk kop kow kowlp kowlp*.
Status: common summer resident.
Habitat: semi-open deciduous habitats; dense tangles and thickets at the edges of orchards, urban parks, agricultural fields, woodlots and windbreaks.

Similar Birds

Black-billed Cuckoo

Mourning Dove (p. 94)

Yellow-billed Cuckoo

- yellow eye ring
- rufous tinge on primaries
- mainly yellow, slightly down-curved bill with black upper ridge
- long tail with large white spots on underside

Nesting: on a low horizontal branch in a deciduous shrub or small tree; flimsy platform nest of twigs is lined with grass; pale bluish green eggs are 1¼ x ⅞ in; pair incubates 3–4 eggs for 9–11 days.

Did You Know?

The Yellow-billed Cuckoo, or "Rain Crow," has a propensity for calling on dark, cloudy days and a reputation for predicting rainstorms.

Look For

Yellow-billed Cuckoos lay larger clutches when outbreaks of cicadas or tent caterpillars provide an abundant food supply.

Greater Roadrunner
Geococcyx californianus

Celebrated for its appearance, speed and ability to catch rattlesnakes, the Greater Roadrunner is one of Oklahoma's most fascinating birds. This terrestrial member of the cuckoo family runs on spindly legs at speeds of up to 17 miles per hour, chasing after the small rodents, lizards, scorpions and insects that make up its varied diet. Lightning quick reflexes allow the roadrunner to also snatch hummingbirds, bats and rattlesnakes, which are repeatedly slammed against the ground and then consumed. Since the roadrunner's carnivorous diet has a high water content, this birds is able survive even if water is not readily available.

Other ID: streaky brown and whitish plumage; bare, blue and red skin patch through eye; short, rounded wings.
Size: *L* 23 in; *W* 22 in.
Voice: descending, dove-like cooing; loud bill-clattering.
Status: uncommon resident.
Habitat: open arid areas, thickets, brushy wooded areas, agricultural land, sometimes in towns.

Similar Birds

Ring-necked Pheasant (female)

Look For

This bird is commonly seen dashing along and across highways and gravel roads. Its zygodactyl feet leave X-shaped tracks.

Greater Roadrunner 99

raised head crest

long, thick bill with hooked tip

very long tail

powerful, scaly legs

Nesting: usually in a cactus, dense shrub or low tree; cup-shaped stick nest is lined with vegetation and feathers (may include snakeskin and dried cow manure); white eggs are 1½ x 1¼ in; pair incubates 3–6 eggs for 20 days; may mate for life and defend breeding territory year-round.

Did You Know?

This bird usually swallows its prey whole, even a snake that is too long to consume completely. The roadrunner will continue about its business with the tail of the snake hanging out of its bill, gradually swallowing the rest of its meal as the other end is digested.

Eastern Screech-Owl
Megascops asio

red morph

The small Eastern Screech-Owl is a year-round resident of low-elevation, deciduous woodlands, though its presence is rarely detected. It usually sleeps away the daylight hours, but excited calls from a mobbing horde of chickadees or a squawking gang of Blue Jays can alert you to an owl's daytime presence. Small birds that mob a screech-owl often do so after losing a family member during the night.
• Eastern Screech-Owls have two color morphs, a red and a gray, of which the gray morph is more common in Oklahoma.

Other ID: reddish or grayish overall; yellow eyes.
Size: *L* 8–9 in; *W* 20–22 in.
Voice: horselike "whinny" that rises and falls.
Status: uncommon year-round resident.
Habitat: mature deciduous forests, open deciduous and riparian woodlands, orchards and shade trees with natural cavities.

Similar Birds

Northern Saw-whet Owl

Long-eared Owl

Western Screech-Owl

Eastern Screech-Owl 101

short "ear" tufts

dark breast streaking

gray morph

Nesting: in an unlined natural cavity or artificial nest box; white eggs are 1½ x 1¼ in; female incubates 4–5 eggs for about 26 days; male brings food to the female during incubation.

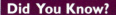

Did You Know?

The Eastern Screech-Owl has one of the most varied diets of any owl and will capture small animals, earthworms, insects and even fish.

Look For

The nearly identical Western Screech-Owl, best differentiated by its call, resides in Cimarron County at the western end of the Panhandle.

Great Horned Owl
Bubo virginianus

This highly adaptable and superbly camouflaged hunter has sharp hearing and powerful vision that allow it to hunt at night as well as by day. It will swoop down from a perch onto almost any small creature that moves. • An owl has specially designed feathers on its wings to reduce noise. The leading edge of the flight feathers is fringed rather than smooth, which interrupts airflow over the wing and allows the owl to fly silently. • Great Horned Owls begin their courtship as early as January, and by February and March the females are already incubating their eggs.

Other ID: overall plumage varies from light gray to dark brown; heavily mottled, gray, brown and black upperparts; yellow eyes; white chin.
Size: *L* 18–25 in; *W* 3–5 ft.
Voice: breeding call is 4–6 deep hoots: *hoo-hoo-hoooo hoo-hoo* or *Who's awake? Me too;* female gives higher-pitched hoots.
Status: uncommon year-round resident.
Habitat: fragmented forests, fields, riparian woodlands, suburban parks and wooded edges of clearings.

Similar Birds

Long-eared Owl

Barred Owl
(p. 104)

Great Horned Owl 103

tall, widely spaced "ear" tufts form a triangle with beak

rusty orange facial disc is outlined in black

fine, horizontal barring on breast

Nesting: in another bird's abandoned stick nest or in a tree cavity; adds little or no nest material; dull whitish eggs are 2¼ x 1⅞ in; mostly the female incubates 2–3 eggs for 28–35 days.

Did You Know?

The Great Horned Owl has a poor sense of smell, which might explain why it is the only consistent predator of skunks.

Look For

Owls regurgitate pellets that contain the indigestible parts of their prey. You can find these pellets, which are generally clean and dry, under frequently used perches.

Barred Owl
Strix varia

The adaptable Barred Owl is found in many woodland habitats, especially those near water. It prefers large tracts of mature forest, ranging from swampy bottomlands to higher mixed forests. • Each spring, the escalating laughs, hoots and gargling howls of Barred Owls reinforce the pair bond. They tend to be most vocal during late evening and early morning when the moon is full, the air is calm and the sky is clear. • Four other owls lacking "ear" tufts occur in Oklahoma, but they use habitats quite different from that of the Barred Owl.

Other ID: mottled, dark gray-brown plumage; no "ear" tufts.
Size: *L* 17–24 in; *W* 3½–4 ft.
Voice: loud, hooting, rhythmic, laughing call is heard mostly in spring: *Who cooks for you? Who cooks for you all?*
Status: uncommon resident in eastern Oklahoma; rare in the west.
Habitat: mature forests, especially in dense stands near streams, rivers and lakes.

Similar Birds

Burrowing Owl

Short-eared Owl

Barn Owl

Barred Owl

- dark eyes
- pale bill
- horizontal barring around neck and upper breast
- vertical streaking on belly

Nesting: in a natural tree cavity, broken tree-top or abandoned stick nest; adds very little material to the nest; white eggs are 2 x 1⅝ in; female incubates 2–3 eggs for 28–33 days.

Did You Know?

In darkness, the Barred Owl's eyesight may be 100 times keener than that of humans, and it is able to locate and follow prey using sound alone.

Look For

Dark eyes make the Barred Owl unique—most familiar large owls in North America have yellow eyes.

Common Nighthawk
Chordeiles minor

The Common Nighthawk makes an unforgettable booming sound as it flies high overhead. In an energetic courting display, the male dives, then swerves skyward, making a hollow *vroom* sound with its wings. • Like other members of the nightjar family, the Common Nighthawk has adapted to catch insects in midair: its large, gaping mouth is surrounded by feather shafts that funnel insects into its bill. A nighthawk can eat over 2600 insects in one day, including mosquitoes, blackflies and flying ants. • Look for nighthawks foraging for insects at nighttime baseball games.

Other ID: *Male:* white throat. *In flight:* shallowly forked, barred tail; erratic flight.
Size: *L* 8–10 in; *W* 23–26 in.
Voice: frequently repeated, nasal *peent peent*.
Status: common summer resident.
Habitat: *Breeding:* forest openings, rocky outcroppings and gravel rooftops. *In migration:* often near water; any area with large numbers of flying insects.

Similar Birds

Chuck-will's-widow

Whip-poor-will

Common Poorwill

Common Nighthawk 107

- bold, white "wrist" patches on long, pointed wings
- very small bill
- cryptic, mottled plumage
- barred underparts

Nesting: on bare ground; no nest is built; heavily marked, creamy white to buff eggs are 1⅛ x ⅞ in; female incubates 2 eggs for about 19 days; both adults feed the young.

Did You Know?

It was once believed that members of the nightjar, or "goatsucker," family could suck milk from the udders of goats, causing the goats to go blind!

Look For

With their short legs and tiny feet, Nighthawks sit lengthwise on tree branches and blend in perfectly with the bark.

Chimney Swift
Chaetura pelagica

Chimney Swifts are the "frequent fliers" of the bird world—they feed, drink, bathe, collect nest material and even mate while they fly! They spend much of their time catching insects in the skies, high above the treetops. During night migrations, swifts sleep as they fly, relying on changing wind conditions to steer them. • Chimney Swifts have small, weak legs and cannot take flight again if they land on the ground. For this reason, swifts usually cling to vertical surfaces with their strong claws.

Other ID: brown overall; slim body. *In flight:* rapid wingbeats; boomerang-shaped profile; erratic flight pattern.
Size: *L* 5–5½ in; *W* 12–13 in.
Voice: call is a rapid *chitter-chitter-chitter,* given in flight; also gives a rapid series of staccato *chip* notes.
Status: common summer resident.
Habitat: forages above cities and towns; roosts and nests in chimneys; may nest in tree cavities in more remote areas.

Similar Birds

Northern Rough-winged Swallow

Bank Swallow

Purple Martin (p. 142)

Chimney Swift

long, thin, pointed, crescent-shaped wings

squared tail

Nesting: often colonial; half-saucer nest of short twigs is attached to a vertical wall using saliva; white eggs are ¾ x ½ in; pair incubates 4–5 eggs for 19–21 days.

Did You Know?

Migrating Chimney Swifts may fly as high as 10,000 feet; above this altitude aircraft are required to carry oxygen.

Look For

In early evenings during migration, Chimney Swifts are often seen in high numbers swirling above large, old chimneys before they enter to roost for the night.

Ruby-throated Hummingbird
Archilochus colubris

Ruby-throated Hummingbirds feed on sweet, energy-rich flower nectar and pollinate flowers in the process. You can attract hummingbirds to your backyard with a red nectar feeder filled with a sugarwater solution (red food coloring is both unnecessary and harmful to the birds) or with tubular, nectar-producing flowers such as honeysuckle or bee balm. • Each year, Ruby-throated Hummingbirds migrate across the Gulf of Mexico—a nonstop, 500-mile journey.

Other ID: thin, needle-like bill; pale underparts.
Size: *L* 3½–4 in; *W* 4–4½ in.
Voice: a loud *chick* and other high squeaks; soft buzzing of the wings while in flight.
Status: common summer resident in the east and central regions; rare in the west.
Habitat: open, mixed woodlands, wetlands, orchards, tree-lined meadows, flower gardens and backyards with trees and feeders.

Similar Birds

Black-chinned Hummingbird

Rufous Hummingbird

Broad-tailed Hummingbird

Ruby-throated Hummingbird

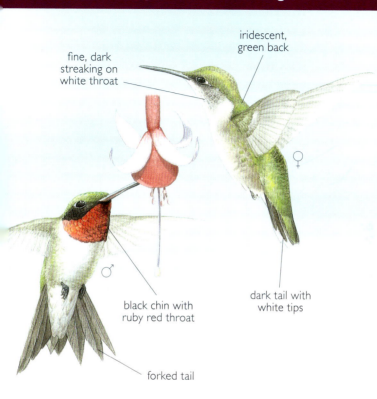

- iridescent, green back
- fine, dark streaking on white throat
- dark tail with white tips
- black chin with ruby red throat
- forked tail

Nesting: on a horizontal tree limb; tiny, deep cup nest of plant down and fibers is held together with spider silk; lichens and leaves are pasted on the exterior walls; white eggs are ½ x ⅜ in; female incubates 2 eggs for 13–16 days.

Did You Know?

In straight-ahead flight, hummingbirds beat their wings up to 80 times per second, and their hearts can beat up to 1200 times per minute!

Look For

Several other species of hummingbirds that nest in the Rocky Mountains migrate across western Oklahoma in fall and can be looked for in August and September.

Belted Kingfisher
Ceryle alcyon

Perched on a bare branch over a productive pool, the Belted Kingfisher utters a scratchy, rattling call. Then, with little regard for its scruffy hairdo, the "king of the fishers" plunges headfirst into the water, snatching a fish or a frog. Back at its perch, the kingfisher flips its prey into the air and swallows it headfirst. Much like an owl, a kingfisher will regurgitate the indigestible portion of its food as pellets that accumulate beneath its favorite perches. • Nestlings have closed eyes and are featherless for the first week, but after five days they are able to swallow small fish whole.

Other ID: bluish upperparts; small, white patch near eye; straight bill; short legs; white underwings.
Size: *L* 11–14 in; *W* 20–21 in.
Voice: fast, repetitive, cackling rattle, like a teacup shaking on a saucer.
Status: uncommon resident.
Habitat: rivers, large streams, lakes, marshes and beaver ponds, especially near exposed soil banks, gravel pits or bluffs.

Similar Birds

Blue Jay
(p. 136)

Look For

With an extra reddish brown band across her belly, the female kingfisher is more colorful than her mate.

Belted Kingfisher 113

- shaggy crest
- white collar
- ♀
- ♂
- blue-gray breast band
- rust-colored belt on female may be incomplete

Nesting: in a cavity at the end of an earth burrow; glossy white eggs are 1 3/8 x 1 in; pair incubates 6–7 eggs for 22–24 days.

Did You Know?

Kingfisher pairs nest on sandy banks, taking turns digging a tunnel with their sturdy bills and claws. Nest burrows may measure up to 6 ft. long and are often found near water. Once the young are at least five days old, the parents return to the nest regularly with small fingerling fish.

Red-headed Woodpecker

Melanerpes erythrocephalus

Red-heads were previously common throughout their range, but their numbers have declined dramatically over the past century. Since the introduction of the European Starling, Red-headed Woodpeckers have been forced to compete for scarce nesting cavities. • These birds are frequent traffic fatalities, often struck by vehicles when they dart from their perches and over roadways to catch flying insects.

Other ID: black tail; white underparts.
Juvenile: brown head, back, wings and tail; slight brown streaking on white underparts.
Size: *L* 9–9½ in; *W* 17 in.
Voice: loud series of *kweer* or *kwrring* notes; occasionally a chattering *kerr-r-ruck;* also drums softly in short bursts.
Status: common summer resident; winter status depends upon availability of food, especially acorns.
Habitat: open deciduous woodlands (especially oak woodlands), urban parks, river edges and roadsides with groves of scattered trees.

Similar Birds

Pileated Woodpecker   Red-bellied Woodpecker
                         (p. 116)

Red-headed Woodpecker 115

- bright red head
- black back and wings
- white rump and inner wing patches
- *juvenile*
- large, white patch on wing

Nesting: male excavates a nest cavity in a dead tree or limb; white eggs are 1 x ¾ in; pair incubates 4–5 eggs for 12–13 days; both adults feed the young.

Did You Know?

This bird's scientific name *erythrocephalus* means "red head" in Greek.

Look For

Many woodpeckers have zygodactyl feet—two toes point forward and two point back—which allows them to move vertically up and down tree trunks.

Red-bellied Woodpecker

Melanerpes carolinus

This widespread bird is no stranger to suburban backyards and is found year-round in woodlands throughout the eastern states, but numbers fluctuate depending on habitat availability and weather conditions. • Unlike most woodpeckers, Red-bellies consume large amounts of plant material such as berries and seeds, seldom excavating wood for insects. • When occupying an area together with Red-headed Woodpeckers, Red-bellies will nest in the trunk, below the foliage, and the Red-heads will nest in dead branches among the foliage.

Other ID: reddish tinge on belly. *Juvenile:* dark gray crown; streaked breast.
Size: *L* 9–10½ in; *W* 16 in.
Voice: call is a soft, rolling *churr;* drums in second-long bursts.
Status: common resident except in the Panhandle.
Habitat: mature deciduous woodlands; occasionally in wooded residential areas.

Similar Birds

Northern Flicker (p. 120)

Yellow-bellied Sapsucker

Golden-fronted Woodpecker

Red-bellied Woodpecker 117

Nesting: in woodlands or residential areas; in a cavity excavated by mainly by the male; may use a nest box; white eggs are 1 x ¾ in; pair incubates 4–5 eggs for 12–14 days.

Did You Know?

Studies of banded Red-bellied Woodpeckers have shown that these birds have a life span in the wild of more than 20 years.

Look For

The Red-bellied Woodpecker's namesake, its red belly, is only a small reddish area that is difficult to see in the field.

Downy Woodpecker

Picoides pubescens

A bird feeder well stocked with peanut butter and black-oil sunflower seeds may attract a pair of Downy Woodpeckers to your backyard. These approachable little birds are more tolerant of human activity than most other species, and they visit feeders more often than the larger, more aggressive Hairy Woodpeckers *(P. villosus)*. • Like other woodpeckers, the Downy has evolved special features to help cushion the shock of repeated hammering, including a strong bill and neck muscles, a flexible, reinforced skull and a brain that is tightly packed in its protective cranium.

Other ID: black eye line and crown; white belly. *Male:* small, red patch on back of head. *Female:* no red patch.
Size: *L* 6–7 in; *W* 12 in.
Voice: long, unbroken trill; calls are a sharp *pik* or *ki-ki-ki* or whiny *queek queek*.
Status: common year-round resident.
Habitat: any wooded environment, especially deciduous and mixed forests and areas with tall, deciduous shrubs.

Similar Birds

Hairy Woodpecker

Ladder-backed Woodpecker

Downy Woodpecker 119

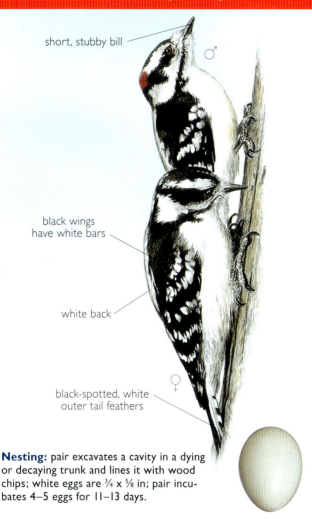

- short, stubby bill
- ♂
- black wings have white bars
- white back
- black-spotted, white outer tail feathers
- ♀

Nesting: pair excavates a cavity in a dying or decaying trunk and lines it with wood chips; white eggs are ¾ x ⅝ in; pair incubates 4–5 eggs for 11–13 days.

Did You Know?

Woodpeckers have feathered nostrils, which filter out the sawdust produced by hammering.

Look For

Downy Woodpeckers and Hairy Woodpeckers have white outer tail feathers, but the Downy's have several dark spots while the Hairy's are pure white.

Northern Flicker
Colaptes auratus

Instead of boring holes in trees, the Northern Flicker scours the ground in search of invertebrates, particularly ants. With robinlike hops, it investigates anthills, grassy meadows and forest clearings. • Flickers often bathe in dusty depressions. The dust particles absorb oils and bacteria that can harm the birds' feathers. To clean themselves even more thoroughly, flickers squash ants and preen themselves with the remains. Ants contain formic acid, which kills small parasites on the birds' skin and feathers.

Other ID: long bill; brownish to buff face; gray crown; white rump. *Male:* black "mustache" stripe. *Female:* no "mustache."
Size: *L* 12–13 in; *W* 20 in.
Voice: loud, rapid, laughlike *kick-kick-kick-kick-kick-kick; woika-woika-woika* issued during courtship.
Status: common migrant and winter resident; uncommon in summer.
Habitat: *Breeding:* open woodlands and forest edges, fields, meadows, beaver ponds and other wetlands. *In migration* and *winter:* urban gardens.

Similar Birds

Red-bellied Woodpecker (p. 116)

Yellow-bellied Sapsucker

Norther Flicker 121

- barred, brown back and wings
- brownish cheeks
- ♂
- black-spotted, buff to whitish underparts
- red nape crescent
- black "bib"
- ♀
- yellow underwings and undertail

Nesting: pair excavates a cavity in a dying or decaying trunk and lines it with wood chips; may also use a nest box; white eggs are 1⅛ x ⅞ in; pair incubates 5–8 eggs for 11–16 days.

Did You Know?

The very long tongue of a woodpecker wraps around twin structures in the skull and is stored like a measuring tape in its case.

Look For

Flickers with red (rather than yellow) underwings and undertail coverts can be seen in late fall and winter, particularly in western Oklahoma.

Least Flycatcher

Empidonax minimus

The Least Flycatcher is the most common migrant *Empidonax* flycatcher in Oklahoma, and it is the only one that most birders confidently identify based on plumage alone. Its bold white eye ring and clear white wing bars stand out at close view. Like other flycatchers, these little birds are olive-brown above and pale below, but they lack the obvious yellow tones of other flycatchers. Their call is a clear, sharp *whit*. • Eight species of *Empidonax* flycatchers have been found in Oklahoma. The best way to identify them is by their vocalizations.

Other ID: white throat; olive brown upperparts; gray breast; gray-white to yellowish belly and undertail coverts; fairly long, narrow tail.
Size: L 4½–5½ in; W 7½–8 in.
Voice: song is a constantly repeated, dry *che-bek che-bek*.
Status: common migrant in the east; rare migrant in the west.
Habitat: open deciduous or mixed woodlands; forest openings and edges; often in second-growth woodlands and occasionally near human habitation.

Similar Birds

Eastern Wood-Pewee

Willow Flycatcher

Acadian Flycatcher

Least Flycatcher 123

- bold, white eye ring
- 2 white wing bars
- mostly dark bill has yellow-orange lower base

Nesting: does not nest in Oklahoma; nests in northern U.S. and Canada; in the crotch or fork of a small tree or shrub, often against the trunk; female builds a small cup nest of plant fibers and bark; creamy white eggs are ⅝ x ½ in; female incubates 4 eggs for 13–15 days.

Did You Know?

Empidonax flycatchers are aptly named: the literal translation is "mosquito king" and refers to their insect-hunting prowess.

Look For

A feeding flycatcher will sit on a branch, launch out suddenly to snap up an insect, and then circle back to land on the same perch.

Eastern Phoebe
Sayornis phoebe

Whether you are poking around a barnyard, a campground picnic shelter or your backyard shed, there is a very good chance you will stumble upon an Eastern Phoebe family and its marvelous mud nest. The Eastern Phoebe's nest building and territorial defense is normally well underway by the time most other songbirds arrive in Oklahoma in late April and May. Once limited to nesting on natural cliffs and fallen riparian trees, this adaptive flycatcher has found success nesting in culverts and under bridges and eaves, especially when water is near. Look for it around such structures.

Other ID: gray-brown upperparts; belly may have yellow wash in fall; no eye ring; faint wing bars; dark legs.
Size: *L* 6½–7 in; *W* 10½ in.
Voice: song is a hearty, snappy *fee-bee*, delivered frequently; call is a sharp *chip*.
Status: common summer resident in the east; uncommon in the west; rare in winter.
Habitat: open deciduous woodlands, forest edges and clearings; usually near water.

Similar Birds

Vermilion Flycatcher (female)

Olive-sided Flycatcher

Say's Phoebe

Eastern Phoebe 125

- all-black crown and bill
- gray wash on breast and sides
- white underparts
- *breeding*
- frequently pumps its tail

Nesting: under the ledge of a building, picnic shelter, bridge or in a culvert, cliff or well; cup-shaped mud nest is lined with soft material; unmarked, white eggs are ¾ x 9/16 in; female incubates 4–5 eggs for about 16 days.

Did You Know?

Eastern Phoebes sometimes reuse their nest sites for many years. Females that save energy by reusing a nest are often able to lay more eggs.

Look For

Some other birds pump their tails while perched, but few species can match the zest and frequency of the Eastern Phoebe's tail pumping.

Great Crested Flycatcher

Myiarchus crinitus

Loud, raucous calls give away the presence of the brightly colored Great Crested Flycatcher. Unlike other eastern flycatchers, the Great Crested prefers to nest in a tree cavity or abandoned woodpecker hole, or sometimes uses a nest box intended for a bluebird. Once in a while, the Great Crested Flycatcher will decorate the nest entrance with a shed snakeskin; if none is available it may substitute translucent plastic wrap. The purpose of this practice is not fully understood, though it may serve as a warning to potential predators.

Other ID: dark olive brown upperparts; heavy, black bill.
Size: *L* 8–9 in; *W* 13 in.
Voice: loud, whistled *wheep!* and a rolling *prrrrreet!*
Status: common summer resident but less common in the Panhandle.
Habitat: deciduous and mixed woodlands and forests, usually near openings or edges.

Similar Birds

Olive-sided Flycatcher

Ash-throated Flycatcher

Great Crested Flycatcher 127

- peaked, "crested" head
- gray throat and upper breast
- bright yellow belly and undertail coverts
- reddish brown tail

Nesting: in a tree cavity or artificial cavity lined with grass; may hang a shed snakeskin over entrance hole; heavily marked, pale buff eggs are 7/8 x 5/8 in; female incubates 5 eggs for 13–15 days.

Did You Know?

Many animals and birds depend on tree cavities for shelter. A large, dead tree can often be just as beneficial for birds as a living one.

Look For

Follow the loud the loud *wheep!* calls and watch for a show of bright yellow and rufous feathers to find this flycatcher.

Western Kingbird
Tyrannus verticalis

Kingbirds perch on wires or fence posts in open habitats and fearlessly chase larger birds from their breeding territories. Once you have witnessed a kingbird's brave attacks against much larger birds, such as crows and hawks, you'll understand why this rabble-rouser was awarded its regal common name. • The tumbling aerial courtship display of the Western Kingbird is a good indication that this bird might be breeding. The male twists and turns as he rises to heights of 65 feet above the ground, stalls, then tumbles and flips his way back to the earth.

Other ID: black bill; faint, dark gray mask; thin, orange crown (rarely seen); pale gray breast; black tail; white edges on outer tail feathers.
Size: L 8–9 in; W 15½ in.
Voice: chatty, twittering *whit-ker-whit;* also a short *kit* or extended *kit-kit-keetle-dot.*
Status: abundant summer resident in the west, becoming less common eastward.
Habitat: open, dry country; grassy areas with scattered brush or hedgerows; edges of open fields; riparian woodlands.

Similar Birds

Great Crested Flycatcher (p. 126)

Cassin's Kingbird

Western Kingbird 129

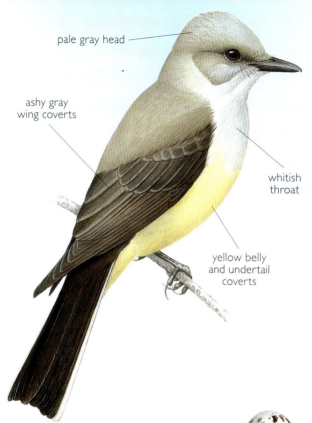

- pale gray head
- ashy gray wing coverts
- whitish throat
- yellow belly and undertail coverts

Nesting: in a deciduous tree or on a utility pole; bulky cup nest of grass and twigs is lined with soft material; whitish, heavily blotched eggs are 7/8 x 5/8 in; female incubates 3–5 eggs for 18–19 days.

Did You Know?

The scientific descriptor *verticalis* refers to the bird's hidden orange crown patch, which is flared during courtship and in combat.

Look For

A Western Kingbird will capture insects flushed by a lawnmower. It may chase an insect for up to 50 feet before a capture is made.

Eastern Kingbird
Tyrannus tyrannus

Sometimes referred to as the "Jekyll and Hyde Bird," the Eastern Kingbird is a gregarious fruit eater while wintering in South America, and an antisocial, aggressive insect eater while nesting in North America. • The Eastern Kingbird fearlessly attacks crows, hawks and even humans that pass through its territory, pursuing and pecking at them until the threat has passed. No one familiar with this bird's pugnacious behavior will refute its scientific name, *Tyrannus tyrannus*. This bird reveals a gentler side of its character in its quivering, butterfly-like courtship flight.

Other ID: black bill and legs; no eye ring; white underparts; grayish breast; white-tipped tail.
Size: *L* 8½–9 in; *W* 15 in.
Voice: call is a quick, loud, chattering *kit-kit-kitter-kitter;* also a buzzy *dzee-dzee-dzee.*
Status: common summer resident.
Habitat: fields with scattered shrubs, trees or hedgerows, forest fringes, clearings, shrubby roadsides, towns and farmyards.

Similar Birds

Tree Swallow

Eastern Phoebe
(p. 124)

Eastern Kingbird 131

- thin, orange-red crown (rarely seen)
- small head crest
- dark gray to black upperparts

Nesting: on a horizontal limb, stump or upturned tree root; cup nest is made of weeds, twigs and grass; darkly blotched, white to pinkish white eggs are 1 x ¾ in; female incubates 3–4 eggs for 14–18 days.

Did You Know?

Eastern Kingbirds rarely walk or hop on the ground—they prefer to fly, even for very short distances.

Look For

Eastern Kingbirds are common and widespread in Oklahoma. On a drive in the country you will likely spot at least one of these birds sitting on a fence or utility wire.

Scissor-tailed Flycatcher
Tyrannus forficatus

Endowed with the refined, long tail feathers of a tropical bird of paradise, the Scissor-tailed Flycatcher tops many birders' "must-see" lists. This lovely bird often perches on roadside fences or utility wires, allowing observers to marvel at its beauty and grace. • After the breeding season, stray Scissor-tailed Flycatchers wander nationwide and may turn up well away from their normal breeding range. • The Scissor-tailed Flycatcher is Oklahoma's state bird.

Other ID: dark wings; whitish to grayish head, back and breast; bright pink "wing pits"; *Immature:* duller, shorter-tailed version of adult; brownish back.
Size: *L* 10 in; adult male up to 15 in (including tail); *W* 15 in.
Voice: calls include a repeated *ka-leap* and a sharp, harsh *kek*.
Status: common summer resident, except uncommon in the far west and southeast.
Habitat: grasslands, pastures, roadsides and semi-open country.

Look For

The name "Scissor-tailed" is derived from the male's habit of opening and closing the gap between his long tail feathers during courtship flight. The roller coaster-like courtship ritual often includes dazzling backward somersaults that enhance the beauty of the male's streaming tail.

Scissor-tailed Flycatcher 133

salmon pink flanks and lower underparts

salmon pink underwing linings

extremely long outer tail feathers that give a forked appearance in flight

Nesting: in a tree, shrub or on a utility pole or ledge; female builds a messy cup nest of twigs, vegetation, string and animal hair; brown-blotched, whitish eggs are 7/8 x 5/8 in; female incubates 3–5 eggs for 12–14 days.

Did You Know?

Scissor-tailed Flycatchers will attack a variety of other bird species, including hawks, vultures, crows and sparrows, to defend their breeding territory. Raptors and crows are often chased by multiple flycatchers, who may also peck at their backs to drive them away.

Loggerhead Shrike
Lanius ludovicianus

The Loggerhead Shrike is truly in a class of its own. This predatory songbird has very acute vision, and it often perches atop trees and on wires to scan for small prey, which is caught in fast, direct flight or a swooping dive. • A male will display his hunting prowess by impaling prey on thorns or barbed wire, earning this bird the nickname "Butcherbird." • Many shrikes are killed by traffic as they fly low across roads to prey on insects attracted to the warm pavement. • The Northern Shrike is a rare winter visitor to northern and western Oklahoma.

Other ID: gray crown and back; white underparts. *In flight:* white wing patches; white-edged tail.
Size: *L* 9 in; *W* 12 in.
Voice: a high-pitched, hiccupy *bird-ee bird-ee* in summer; infrequently a harsh *shack-shack* year-round.
Status: uncommon summer resident; more common in migration and winter.
Habitat: grazed pastures and marginal and abandoned farmlands with scattered hawthorn shrubs, fence posts, barbed wire and nearby wetlands.

Similar Birds

Northern Shrike

Northern Mockingbird (p. 166)

Loggerhead Shrike 135

black mask extends above hooked bill onto forehead

thick, hooked bill

whitish throat patch

black tail and wings

Nesting: low in a shrub or small tree; bulky cup nest of twigs and grass is lined with animal hair, feathers and plant down; darkly blotched, pale buff to grayish white eggs are 1 x ¾ in; female incubates 5–6 eggs for 15–17 days.

Did You Know?

Habitat loss has contributed to a steady decline in Loggerhead Shrike populations, earning this bird endangered species status in North America.

Look For

Shrikes typically perch at the top of tall trees to survey the surrounding area for prey.

Blue Jay
Cyanocitta cristata

The Blue Jay is a familiar sight throughout Oklahoma. White-flecked wing feathers and sharply defined facial features make this bird easy to recognize. • Jays can be quite aggressive when competing for sunflower seeds and peanuts at backyard feeding stations, and they rarely hesitate to drive away smaller birds, squirrels or even threatening cats. Even the Great Horned Owl is not too formidable a predator for a group of these brave, boisterous mobsters to harass.

Other ID: blue upperparts; white underparts; black bill.
Size: *L* 11–12 in; *W* 16 in.
Voice: noisy, screaming *jay-jay-jay;* nasal *queedle queedle queedle-queedle* sounds like a muted trumpet; often imitates various sounds, including calls of other birds.
Status: common resident and abundant migrant, but less common in the west.
Habitat: mixed deciduous forests, agricultural areas, scrubby fields and townsites.

Similar Birds

Western Scrub-Jay

Steller's Jay

Pinyon Jay

Blue Jay 137

- blue crest
- black "necklace"
- dark bars and white flecking on wings
- dark bars and white corners on blue tail

Nesting: in a tree or tall shrub; pair builds a bulky stick nest; greenish, buff or pale eggs, spotted with gray and brown, are 1⅛ x ¾ in; pair incubates 4–5 eggs for 16–18 days.

Did You Know?

Blue Jays store food from feeders in trees and other places for later use.

Look For

Three close relatives from the western U.S., the Steller's Jay, Western Scrub-Jay and Pinyon Jay, occasionally visit western Oklahoma in fall and winter.

American Crow
Corvus brachyrhynchos

The familiar "caw" that most often emanates from this treetop squawker seems unrepresentative of its intelligence. However, this wary, clever bird is also an impressive mimic, able to whine like a dog and laugh or cry like a human. • Members of the highly social Corvid family are among the most clever birds. They have superb memories and are able to learn, make simple tools and solve problems. Crows will often drop walnuts or clams from great heights onto a hard surface to crack the shells, one of the few examples of birds using objects to manipulate food. • The nearly identical Fish Crow is found near water and can be best identified by its high, nasal call.

Other ID: black bill and legs; short, square-shaped tail.
Size: *L* 17–21 in; *W* 3 ft.
Voice: distinctive, far-carrying, repetitive *caw-caw-caw*.
Status: common resident.
Habitat: urban areas, agricultural fields and other open areas with scattered woodlands.

Similar Birds

Chihuahuan Raven

Common Raven

Black-billed Magpie

American Crow 139

slim, sleek head and throat

glossy, purple black plumage

Nesting: in a tree or on a utility pole; large stick-and-branch nest is lined with fur and soft plant material; darkly blotched, gray-green to blue-green eggs are 1⅝ x 1⅛ in; female incubates 4–6 eggs for about 18 days.

Did You Know?

Crows are family oriented, and the young from the previous year may help their parents to raise the nestlings.

Look For

Large roosts with hundreds of crows may form in towns during winter.

Horned Lark
Eremophila alpestris

The tinkling song of the Horned Lark is always an early sign of spring in Oklahoma. Long before many other birds have returned, the male Horned Lark is already performing his high-speed, plummeting courtship dive. This bird has been known to remain on the nest, protecting its eggs, even during late spring blizzards. • Horned Larks are often abundant at roadsides, searching for seeds, but an approaching vehicle usually sends them flying into an adjacent field. Huge flocks gather in winter, especially in western Oklahoma, and these flocks usually contain longspurs.

Other ID: dark tail with white outer tail feathers. *Male:* light yellow to white face; pale throat; dull brown upperparts. *Female:* duller plumage.
Size: *L* 7 in; *W* 12 in.
Voice: call is a tinkling *tsee-titi* or *zoot;* flight song is a long series of tinkling, twittered whistles.
Status: abundant resident in western and central Oklahoma, uncommon in the east.
Habitat: open areas, including pastures, native prairie, cultivated or sparsely vegetated fields, golf courses and airfields.

Similar Birds

Lapland Longspur (p. 202)

American Pipit

Horned Lark 141

small black "horns" (rarely raised)

black line under eye extends from bill to cheek

black breast band

Nesting: on the ground; in a shallow scrape lined with grass, plant fibers and roots; brown-blotched, gray to greenish white eggs are 1 x 5/8 in; female incubates 3–4 eggs for 10–12 days.

Did You Know?

One way to distinguish a sparrow from a Horned Lark is by their method of travel: Horned Larks walk, but sparrows hop.

Look For

This bird's dark tail contrasts with its light brown body and belly. Look for this feature to identify flying Horned Larks in their open-country habitat.

Purple Martin
Progne subis

These large swallows will entertain you throughout spring and summer if you set up a luxurious "condo complex" for them. You can watch martin adults spiral around their accommodations in pursuit of flying insects, while their young perch clumsily at the cavity openings. Purple Martins once nested in natural tree hollows and in cliff crevices, but now they have virtually abandoned these in favor of human-made housing. • To avoid the invasion of aggressive House Sparrows or European Starlings, it is essential for martin condos to be cleaned out and closed up after each nesting season. Open them again in early April just in time for the returning martins.

Other ID: pointed wings; small bill.
Size: *L* 7–8 in; *W* 18 in.
Voice: rich, fluty, robinlike *pew-pew,* often heard in flight.
Status: common summer resident in the eastern two-thirds of the state; rare in the west.
Habitat: semi-open areas, often near water.

Similar Birds

Tree Swallow

Bank Swallow

Northern Rough-wing Swallow

Purple Martin 143

- glossy, dark blue body
- slightly forked tail
- dark underparts

Nesting: communal; in a birdhouse or a hollowed-out gourd; nest is made of feathers, grass and mud; white eggs are 1 x 5/8 in; female incubates 4–5 eggs for 15–18 days.

Did You Know?

The Purple Martin is North America's largest swallow.

Look For

During late summer before migrating south, hundreds of martins may congregate in the evening to form enormous roosts.

Cliff Swallow
Petrochelidon pyrrhonota

In recent decades Cliff Swallows have expanded their range across North America, nesting on various human-made structures, including bridges, culverts and under eaves. During breeding season, they are common throughout Oklahoma and are often seen catching insects over agricultural fields, marshes, rivers and lakes. • Master mud masons, Cliff Swallows roll mud into balls with their bills and press the pellets together to form their characteristic gourd-shaped nests. Brooding parents peer out of the circular neck of the nest, their gleaming eyes watching the world go by. Their white forehead patch warns intruders that somebody is home.

Other ID: blue-gray wings; buff breast and rump; whitish belly. *In flight:* spotted undertail coverts; nearly square tail.
Size: *L* 5½ in; *W* 13½ in.
Voice: twittering chatter, *churrr-churrr;* also an alarm call, *nyew*.
Status: common throughout Oklahoma but most common in the west.
Habitat: bridges, steep banks, cliffs and buildings, often near watercourses.

Similar Birds

Cave Swallow

Bank Swallow

Northern Rough-winged Swallow

Cliff Swallow 145

- blue-gray cap
- sharply defined, whitish forehead patch
- rusty cheek
- dark throat

Nesting: colonial; under a bridge, on a cliff or under building eaves; pair builds a gourd-shaped mud nest; pale, brown-spotted eggs are ¾ x ⁹⁄₁₆ in; pair incubates 4–5 eggs 14–16 days.

Did You Know?

Cliff Swallows drink on the wing by skimming the water's surface with their open bill.

Look For

This swallow has a square (not forked) tail, cinnamon-colored rump patch and a distinctive flight pattern, ascending with rapid wing-strokes then gliding down.

Barn Swallow
Hirundo rustica

When you encounter this bird, you might first notice its distinctive, deeply forked tail—or you might just find yourself repeatedly ducking to avoid the dives of a protective parent. Barn Swallows once nested on cliffs, but they are now found more frequently nesting on barns, boathouses and under bridges and house eaves. The messy young and aggressive parents unfortunately often motivate people to remove nests just as nesting season is beginning, but this bird's close association with humans allows us to observe the normally secretive reproductive cycle of birds.

Other ID: blue-black upperparts; long, pointed wings.
Size: *L* 7 in; *W* 15 in.
Voice: continuous, twittering chatter: *zip-zip-zip* or *kvick-kvick*.
Status: common migrant and summer resident.
Habitat: open rural and urban areas where bridges, culverts and buildings are found near water.

Similar Birds

Cliff Swallow
(p. 144)

Tree Swallow

Barn Swallow 147

rufous throat and forehead

black "necklace"

rust- to buff-colored underparts

long, deeply forked tail

Nesting: singly or in a small, loose colony; on a human-made structure under an overhang; half or full cup nest is made of mud, grass and straw; brown-spotted, white eggs are ¾ x ½ in; pair incubates 4–7 eggs for 13–17 days.

Did You Know?
The Barn Swallow is a natural pest controller, feeding on insects that are often harmful to crops and livestock.

Look For
During migration and in winter, the gregarious Barn Swallow roosts in enormous flocks. Birds spread out to forage over nearby areas during the day.

Carolina Chickadee
Poecile carolinensis

Fidgety, friendly Carolina Chickadees are familiar to anyone with a backyard feeder well stocked with sunflower seeds and peanut butter. These agile birds even hang upside down to pluck up insects and berries. Like some woodpeckers and nuthatches, the Carolina Chickadee will hoard food for later in the season when food may become scarce. • It's hard to imagine a chickadee using its tiny bill to excavate a nesting cavity, but come breeding season, this energetic little bird can be found hammering out a hollow in a rotting tree. • The similar Mountain Chickadee has a white eye stripe. It is the only chickadee likely to be seen in the western Panhandle.

Other ID: white cheeks; white underparts and buffy flanks.
Size: *L* 4¾ in; *W* 7½ in.
Voice: whistling song has 4 clear notes sounding like *fee-bee fee-bay*.
Status: common resident, except rare in the Panhandle.
Habitat: deciduous and mixed woods, riparian woodlands, groves and isolated shade trees; frequents urban areas.

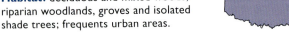

Similar Birds

Blackpoll Warbler   Common Bushtit   Mountain Chickadee

Carolina Chickadee 149

- black cap and "bib"
- grayish nape
- gray upperparts and secondaries

Nesting: excavates or enlarges a tree cavity; may also use nest box; cavity is lined with soft material; white eggs, marked with reddish brown are 9/16 x 7/16 in; female incubates 5–8 eggs for 11–14 days.

Did You Know?

Chickadee flocks are often made up of close family members that vigorously defend the same territory for many generations.

Look For

Outside of the breeding season, chickadees often forage in mixed-species flocks with titmouses, warblers, vireos, kinglets, nuthatches, creepers and small woodpeckers.

Tufted Titmouse
Baeolophus bicolor

This bird's amusing feeding antics and insatiable appetite keep curious observers entertained at bird feeders. Grasping a sunflower seed with its tiny feet, the dexterous Tufted Titmouse will strike its dainty bill repeatedly against the hard outer coating to expose the inner core. • A breeding pair of Tufted Titmice will maintain their bond throughout the year, even when joining small, mixed flocks for the cold winter months. The titmouse family bond is so strong that the young from one breeding season will often stay with their parents long enough to help them with nesting and feeding duties the following year. • The Black-crested Titmouse, a similar species, is found in southwestern Oklahoma.

Other ID: white underparts; pale face.
Size: *L* 6–6½ in; *W* 10 in.
Voice: noisy, scolding call; song is a whistled *peter peter* or *peter peter peter*.
Status: abundant resident in the east, becoming less common westward; rare or absent in the west.
Habitat: deciduous woodlands, groves and suburban parks with large, mature trees.

Similar Birds

Cedar Waxwing (p. 172)

Juniper Titmouse

Tufted Titmouse 151

- black forehead
- gray crest and upperparts
- buffy flanks

Nesting: in a natural cavity or an abandoned woodpecker nest; cavity is lined with soft vegetation, moss and animal hair; brown-speckled, white eggs are 11/16 x 9/16 in; female incubates 5–6 eggs for 12–14 days.

Did You Know?

Nesting pairs search for soft nest lining material in late winter and may accept an offering of the hair that has accumulated in your hairbrush.

Look For

Easily identified by its gray crest and upperparts and black forehead, the tufted titmouse can often be seen at feeders.

White-breasted Nuthatch
Sitta carolinensis

Its upside-down antics and noisy, nasal call make the White-breasted Nuthatch a favorite among novice birders. Whether you spot this black-capped bullet spiraling headfirst down a tree or clinging to the underside of a branch in search of invertebrates, the nuthatch's odd behavior deserves a second glance. • In migration and winter, the White-breasted Nuthatch may be joined at bird feeders by its smaller relative the Red-breasted Nuthatch, especially if pines and other conifer trees are nearby.

Other ID: white underparts and face; straight bill; short legs. *Male:* black cap. *Female:* dark gray cap.
Size: *L* 5½–6 in; *W* 11 in.
Voice: song is a fast, nasal *yank-hank yank-hank*; calls include *ha-ha-ha ha-ha-ha, ank ank* and *ip*.
Status: common resident in the eastern half of the state; uncommon in the west.
Habitat: mixed wood forests, woodlots and backyards.

Similar Birds

Red-breasted Nuthatch

Brown-headed Nuthatch

Pygmy Nuthatch

White-breasted Nuthatch 153

rusty undertail coverts

short tail

gray-blue back

♀

dark crown

♂

Nesting: in a natural cavity or an abandoned woodpecker nest; female lines the cavity with soft material; brown-speckled, white eggs are ¾ x 9/16 in; female incubates 5–8 eggs for 12–14 days.

Did You Know?

Nuthatches are presumably named for their habit of wedging seeds and nuts into crevices and hacking them open with their bills.

Look For

While woodpeckers and creepers use their tails to brace themselves against tree trunks, nuthatches grasp the tree through foot power alone.

Carolina Wren
Thryothorus ludovicianus

The energetic and cheerful Carolina Wren can be shy and retiring, often hiding deep inside dense shrubbery. A nesting Carolina Wren will give intruders a severe scolding, remaining undetectable all the while. Pairs perform lively "duets" at any time of day and in any season. The duet often begins with introductory chatter by the female, followed by ringing variations of *tea-kettle tea-kettle tea-kettle tea* from her mate. • Carolina Wrens readily nest in the brushy thickets of an overgrown backyard or in an obscure nook in a house or barn. If conditions are favorable, two broods may be raised in a single season.

Other ID: white throat; slightly downcurved bill.
Size: *L* 5½ in; *W* 7½ in.
Voice: loud, repetitious *tea-kettle tea-kettle tea-kettle* may be heard at any time of day or year; female often chatters while male sings.
Status: common resident in the east, becoming less common westward.
Habitat: dense forest undergrowth, especially shrubby tangles and thickets.

Similar Birds

House Wren
(p. 156)

Winter Wren

Brown Creeper

Carolina Wren 155

rich brown upperparts including nape and crown

bold white eyebrow

rich, buff-colored underparts

Nesting: in a nest box or natural or artificial cavity; nest is lined with soft material and may include a snakeskin; brown-blotched, white eggs are ¾ x ⁹⁄₁₆ in; female incubates 4–5 eggs for 12–16 days.

Did You Know?

A winter of frigid temperatures can temporarily decimate an otherwise healthy population of Carolina Wrens.

Look For

The best opportunity for viewing this particularly vocal wren is when it sits on a conspicuous perch while unleashing its impressive song.

House Wren
Troglodytes aedon

The bland, nondescript plumage of this suburban and city park dweller can be overlooked until you hear it sing a seemingly unending song in one breath. Despite its bubbly warble, this wren can be very aggressive toward other species that nest in its territory, puncturing and tossing eggs from other bird's nests. A House Wren often builds numerous nests, which later serve as decoys or "dummy" nests to fool would-be enemies. The breeding range of the House Wren has shifted north in recent times leading some people to wonder if it will disappear from the state as a breeding bird.

Other ID: whitish throat; brown upperparts; whitish to buff underparts; faintly barred flanks.
Size: *L* 4½–5 in; *W* 6 in.
Voice: smooth, running, bubbly warble: *tsi-tsi-tsi-tsi oodle-oodle-oodle-oodle*.
Status: uncommon summer resident and migrant.
Habitat: thickets and shrubby openings in or at the edge of deciduous or mixed woodlands; often in shrubs and thickets near buildings.

Similar Birds

Marsh Wren

Winter Wren

Sedge Wren

House Wren 157

- short, upraised tail is finely barred with black
- fine, dark barring on upper wings and lower back
- faint, pale eyebrow and eye ring

Nesting: in a natural or artificial cavity or abandoned woodpecker nest; nest of sticks and grass is lined with feathers and fur; heavily marked, white eggs are ⅝ x ½ in; female incubates 6–8 eggs for 12–15 days.

Did You Know?
This bird has the largest range of any New World passerine, stretching from Canada to southern South America.

Look For
Like all wrens, the House Wren usually carries its short tail raised upward.

Golden-crowned Kinglet
Regulus satrapa

The dainty Golden-crowned Kinglet is not much bigger than a hummingbird and you may just barely hear its high-pitched calls as it gleans for insects, berries and sap in the forest canopy. Its small size exposes it to unique hazards such as perishing on the burrs of burdock plants. • "Pishing" and squeaking sounds often lure these songbirds into an observable range. Behavioral traits, such as its perpetual motion and chronic wing flicking, can help identify Golden-crowns from a distance.

Other ID: black border around crown; black eye line; dark cheek; olive back; darker wings and tail; light underparts.
Size: *L* 4 in; *W* 7 in.
Voice: song is a faint, high-pitched, accelerating *tsee-tsee-tsee-tsee, why do you shilly-shally?*; call is a very high-pitched *tsee tsee tsee*.
Status: uncommon migrant and winter resident.
Habitat: coniferous, deciduous and mixed forests; sometimes visits urban parks and gardens.

Similar Birds

Ruby-crowned Kinglet

Look For

Golden-crowns are often joined by flocks of chickadees, Red-breasted Nuthatches and Brown Creepers at the tops of pines.

Golden-crowned Kinglet 159

Nesting: usually in a spruce or other conifer; hanging nest is made of moss, lichens, twigs and leaves; pale buff eggs, spotted with gray and brown, are ½ x ⅜ in; female incubates 8–9 eggs for 14–15 days.

Did You Know?

Golden-crowned Kinglets spend the winter in areas where nighttime temperatures can fall to below -40° F. To keep warm, they roost communally, use leafy squirrel nests or use hypothermia to regulate body temperature.

Eastern Bluebird
Sialia sialis

The Eastern Bluebird's enticing colors are like those of a warm setting sun against a deep blue sky. • This cavity nester's survival has been put to the test—populations have declined in the presence of the introduced House Sparrow and European Starling which compete with bluebirds for nest sites. The removal of standing dead trees has also diminished nest site availability. Thankfully, bluebird enthusiasts and organizations have developed "bluebird trails," mounting nest boxes on fence posts along highways and rural roads, which has allowed Eastern Bluebird numbers to gradually recover.

Other ID: dark bill and legs. *Female:* thin, white eye ring; gray-brown head and back are tinged with blue; blue wings and tail; paler chestnut underparts.
Size: *L* 7 in; *W* 13 in.
Voice: song is a rich, warbling *turr, turr-lee, turr-lee;* call is a chittering *pew.*
Status: common resident in east and central Oklahoma; uncommon in the far west.
Habitat: fencelines, meadows, fallow fields, forest clearings and edges, golf courses, large lawns and cemeteries.

Similar Birds

Mountain Bluebird

Indigo Bunting
(p. 206)

Blue-gray Gnatcatcher

Eastern Bluebird 161

deep blue upperparts

chestnut red chin, throat and side

♂

white belly and undertail coverts

Nesting: in a natural cavity or nest box; female builds a cup nest of grass, weed stems and small twigs; pale blue eggs are ⅞ x ⅝ in; female incubates 4–5 eggs for 13–16 days.

Did You Know?

This bird's blue color is the result of the microstructure of the feathers, which causes scattering of some wavelengths of light.

Look For

Bluebirds have straight, pointed bills that are perfect for capturing insects. They also feed on berries and are especially attracted to wild grapes, sumac and currants.

American Robin
Turdus migratorius

Come March, the familiar song of the American Robin may wake you early if you are a light sleeper. This abundant bird adapts easily to urban areas and often works from dawn until after dusk when there is a nest to be built or hungry, young mouths to feed. • A hunting robin with its head tilted to the side isn't listening for prey—it is actually looking for movements in the soil. • In winter, fruit trees may attract flocks of robins, which gather to drink the fermenting fruit's intoxicating juices.

Other ID: incomplete, white eye ring; gray-brown back; white undertail coverts.
Size: *L* 10 in; *W* 17 in.
Voice: song is an evenly spaced warble: *cheerily cheer-up cheerio;* call is a rapid *tut-tut-tut*.
Status: common summer resident in east and central Oklahoma, uncommon in the west; common winter resident, sometimes in enormous roosts.
Habitat: *Breeding:* residential lawns and gardens, pastures, urban parks, broken forests, and river shorelines. *Winter:* near fruit-bearing trees and springs.

Similar Birds

Townsend's Solitaire

Hermit Thrush

Swainson's Thrush

American Robin 163

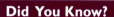

Nesting: in a tree or shrub; cup nest is built of grass, moss, bark and mud; light blue eggs are 1⅛ x ¾ in; female incubates 4 eggs for 11–16 days; raises up to 3 broods per year.

Did You Know?

Robins usually raise two broods per year, and the male cares for the fledglings from the first brood while the female incubates the second clutch of eggs.

Look For

The robin's bright red belly contrasts with its dark head and wings, making this bird easy to identify.

Gray Catbird
Dumetella carolinensis

The Gray Catbird is an accomplished mimic that may fool you as it shuffles through underbrush and dense riparian shrubs, calling its catlike meow. Its mimicking talents are further enhanced by its ability to sing two notes at once, using each side of its syrinx individually.
• The Gray Catbird will vigilantly defend its territory against sparrows, robins, cowbirds and other intruders. It will destroy the eggs and nestlings of other songbirds and will take on an intense defensive posture if approached, screaming and even attempting to hit an intruder.

Other ID: dark gray overall; black eyes, bill and legs.
Size: *L* 8½–9 in; *W* 11 in.
Voice: calls include a catlike *meow* and a harsh *check-check*; song is a variety of warbles, squeaks and mimicked phrases interspersed with a *mew* call.
Status: uncommon summer resident.
Habitat: dense thickets, brambles, shrubby or brushy areas and hedgerows, often near water.

Similar Birds

Northern Mockingbird (p. 166)

Townsend's Solitaire

Gray Catbird

black cap

long tail is dark gray to black

chestnut undertail coverts

Nesting: in a dense shrub or thicket; bulky cup nest is made of twigs, leaves and grass; greenish blue eggs are ⅞ x ⅝ in; female incubates 4 eggs for 12–15 days.

Did You Know?

The watchful female Gray Catbird can recognize a Brown-headed Cowbird egg and will remove it from her nest.

Look For

If you catch a glimpse of this bird during the breeding season, watch the male raise his long slender tail into the air to show off his rust-colored undertail coverts.

Northern Mockingbird

Mimus polyglottos

The Northern Mockingbird has an amazing vocal repertoire that includes over 400 different song types. The male often sings incessantly throughout the breeding season, serenading into the night during a full moon. Mockingbirds can imitate almost anything, including cell phone ring tones and even the sounds made by industrial vehicles. They replicate notes so accurately that even computerized sound analysis is unable to detect the difference between the original source and the mockingbird's imitation.

Other ID: gray upperparts; 2 thin, white wing bars; light gray underparts.
Size: *L* 10 in; *W* 14 in.
Voice: song is a medley of mimicked phrases, often repeated 3–6 times; calls include a harsh *chair* and *chewk*.
Status: common summer resident; less common in winter.
Habitat: hedges, suburban gardens and orchard margins with an abundance of available fruit; hedgerows of roses are especially important in winter.

Similar Birds

Loggerhead Shrike
(p. 134)

Townsend's Solitaire

Northern Mockingbird 167

- long, dark tail with white outer tail feathers
- dark wings
- thin, dark eye line

Nesting: in a small shrub or tree; cup nest is built with twigs and lined with grass and leaves; brown-blotched, bluish gray to greenish eggs are 1 x ⅝ in; female incubates 3–4 eggs for 12–13 days.

Did You Know?

The scientific name *polyglottos* is Greek for "many tongues" and refers to this bird's ability to mimic a wide variety of sounds.

Look For

The Northern Mockingbird's energetic territorial dance is delightful to watch, as males square off in what appears to be a swordless fencing duel.

Brown Thrasher
Toxostoma rufum

The Brown Thrasher shares the streaked breast of a thrush and the long tail of a catbird, but it has a temper all its own. Because it nests close to the ground, the Brown Thrasher defends its nest with a vengeance, attacking snakes and other nest robbers sometimes to the point of drawing blood. • The male Brown Thrasher is capable of producing up to 3000 distinctive song phrases—the most of any North American bird. • The Brown Thrasher is more abundant in the central Great Plains than anywhere else.

Other ID: reddish brown upperparts; long, rufous tail; orange-yellow eyes.
Size: *L* 11½ in; *W* 13 in.
Voice: sings a large variety of phrases, with each phrase usually repeated twice: *dig-it dig-it, hoe-it hoe-it, pull-it-up pull-it-up;* calls include a loud crackling note, a harsh shuck, a soft churr or a whistled, 3-note *pit-cher-ee*.
Status: common summer resident, except rare in the Panhandle; uncommon in winter.
Habitat: dense shrubs and thickets, overgrown pastures, woodland edges and brushy areas; often found in residential areas.

Similar Birds

Hermit Thrush   Curve-billed Thrasher   Wood Thrush

Brown Thrasher

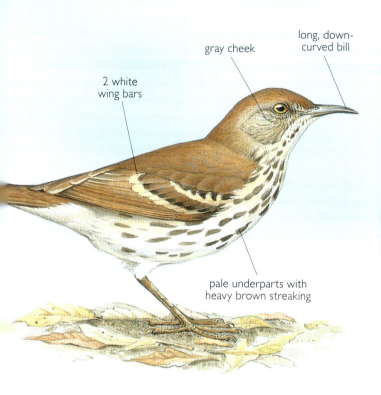

- long, down-curved bill
- gray cheek
- 2 white wing bars
- pale underparts with heavy brown streaking

Nesting: usually in a low shrub; often on the ground; cup nest is made of grass, twigs and leaves; pale blue eggs, dotted with reddish brown, are 1 x ¾ in; pair incubates 4 eggs for 11–14 days.

Did You Know?

Fencing shrubby, wooded areas bordering wetlands and streams can prevent cattle from devastating thrasher nesting habitat.

Look For

You might catch only a flash of rufous as the Brown Thrasher flies from one thicket to another in its shrubby understory habitat.

European Starling
Sturnus vulgaris

The European Starling did not hesitate to make itself known across North America after being released in New York's Central Park in 1890 and 1891. This highly adaptable bird not only took over the nesting sites of native cavity nesters, such as bluebirds and woodpeckers, but it learned to mimic the sounds of Killdeers, Red-tailed Hawks, Northern Bobwhites and meadowlarks. The European Starling is now one of the most common birds in Oklahoma. • European Starlings have a variable diet consisting of Japanese beetles and other destructive agricultural pests, berries, grains and even human food waste.

Other ID: dark eyes; short, squared tail. *Nonbreeding:* feather tips are heavily spotted with white and buff.
Size: *L* 8½ in; *W* 16 in.
Voice: variety of whistles, squeaks and gurgles; imitates other birds.
Status: abundant year-round resident.
Habitat: agricultural areas, towns, woodland edges, landfills and roadsides.

Similar Birds

Rusty Blackbird   Brewer's Blackbird

European Starling

- iridescent, purple-black head, neck and breast
- glossy, green back with buffy spots
- yellow bill
- greenish black underparts

breeding

Nesting: in an abandoned woodpecker cavity, natural cavity or nest box; nest is made of grass, twigs and straw; bluish to greenish white eggs are 1⅛ x ⅞ in; female incubates 4–6 eggs for 12–14 days.

Did You Know?
This bird was brought to New York as part of a society's plan to introduce all the birds mentioned in Shakespeare's writings.

Look For
These birds gather in huge flocks around feedlots or in enormous evening roosts under bridges or on buildings.

Cedar Waxwing
Bombycilla cedrorum

With its black mask and slick hairdo, the Cedar Waxwing has a heroic look. This bird's splendid personality is reflected in its amusing antics after it gorges on fermented berries and in its gentle courtship dance. To court a mate, the gentlemanly male hops toward a female and offers her a berry. The female accepts the berry and hops away, then stops and hops back toward the male to offer him the berry in return. • If a bird's crop is full and it is unable to eat any more, it will continue to pluck fruit and pass it down the line like a bucket brigade, until the fruit is gulped down by a still-hungry bird.

Other ID: brown upperparts; yellow terminal tail band.
Size: *L* 7 in; *W* 12 in.
Voice: faint, high-pitched, trilled whistle: *tseee-tseee-tseee.*
Status: common migrant and winter resident; rare summer resident.
Habitat: wooded residential parks and gardens, overgrown fields, forest edges, second-growth, riparian and open woodlands; often near fruit trees and water.

Similar Birds

Bohemian Waxwing

Look For

The Bohemian Waxwing is a rare winter visitor in Oklahoma. It is larger, grayer, and it has yellow in the wings and rufous undertail coverts.

Cedar Waxwing 173

- cinnamon crest
- black mask
- small red "drops" on wings

Nesting: in a tree or shrub; cup nest is made of twigs, moss and lichen; darkly spotted, bluish to gray eggs are 7/8 x 5/8 in; female incubates 3–5 eggs for 12–16 days.

Did You Know?

Waxwings will show definite signs of tipsiness after consuming fermented fruit.

Orange-crowned Warbler
Vermivora celata

The nondescript Orange-crowned Warbler causes identification problems for many birders. Its drab, olive yellow appearance and lack of field marks makes it frustratingly similar to females of other warbler species, and the male's orange crown patch is seldom visible. • This small warbler has rather deliberate foraging movements, and is usually seen gleaning insects from the leaves and buds of low shrubs. It occasionally eats berries and fruit or visits suet feeders in winter. • The Tennessee Warbler can look similar in fall plumage but is separated by its white undertail coverts.

Other ID: variable plumage; male's orange crown patch is usually hidden. *In flight:* dull olive gray wings and tail.
Size: *L* 5 in; *W* 7 in.
Voice: call is a clear, sharp *chip*.
Status: common migrant; rare winter visitor.
Habitat: any wooded habitat or areas with tall shrubs.

Similar Birds

Tennessee Warbler

Warbling Vireo

Red–eyed Vireo

Orange-crowned Warbler 175

- faint pale eyebrow
- dark eye line that divides the pale eye ring
- greenish gray upperparts
- yellow undertail coverts
- faintly streaked, grayish green underparts

Nesting: does not breed in Oklahoma; breeds in the Arctic; on the ground or occasionally in a low shrub; well-hidden, small cup nest is made of grasses; darkly marked, white eggs are $5/8 \times 1/2$ in; female incubates 4–6 eggs for 12–14 days.

Did You Know?

Vermivora is Latin for "worm-eating" and *celata* is derived from the Latin word for "hidden," a reference to this bird's inconspicuous crown patch.

Look For

Orange-crowned Warblers routinely feed on sap or insects attracted to the sap wells drilled by Yellow-bellied Sapsuckers.

Yellow Warbler
Dendroica petechia

The Yellow Warbler is often parasitized by the Brown-headed Cowbird and can recognize cowbird eggs, but rather than tossing them out, this warbler will build another nest atop the old eggs or abandon the nest completely. Occasionally, cowbirds strike repeatedly, so a five-story nest was once found! The widely distributed Yellow Warbler arrives in May, flitting from branch to branch in search of juicy caterpillars, aphids and beetles and singing its *sweet-sweet* song.

Other ID: bright yellow body; yellowish legs; black bill and eyes. *Female:* may have faint, reddish brown breast streaks.
Size: *L* 5 in; *W* 8 in.
Voice: song is a fast, frequently repeated *sweet-sweet-sweet summer sweet*.
Status: common migrant; uncommon but widespread summer resident.
Habitat: habitat generalist; moist, open woodlands, dense scrub, scrubby meadows, second-growth woodlands, riparian woods and urban parks and gardens.

Similar Birds

Prothonotary Warbler

American Goldfinch

Wilson's Warbler

Yellow Warbler 177

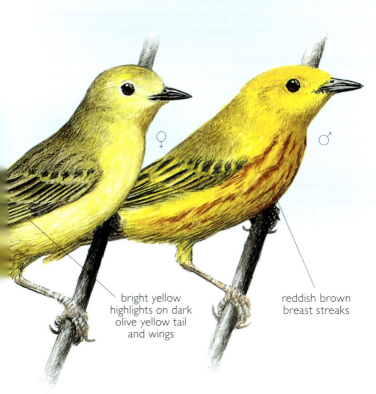

bright yellow highlights on dark olive yellow tail and wings

reddish brown breast streaks

Nesting: in a deciduous tree or shrub; female builds a cup nest of grass, weeds and shredded bark; darkly speckled, greenish white eggs are 5/8 x 1/2 in; female incubates eggs for 11–12 days.

Did You Know?

The Yellow Warbler has an amazing geographical range. It is found throughout North America and on islands in Central and South America.

Look For

These birds favor moist habitats and brushy thickets for breeding but may visit orchards and gardens during migration.

Yellow-rumped Warbler
Dendroica coronata

Yellow-rumped Warblers are the most abundant and widespread wood-warblers in North America. Apple, juniper and sumac trees laden with fruit attract these birds in winter. • This species comes in two forms: the white-throated "Myrtle Warbler" of the East, and the yellow-throated "Audubon's Warbler" of the West. The Myrtle form is commonly found throughout Oklahoma, whereas the Audubon's form is typically found only in extreme western Oklahoma.

Other ID: *Breeding Myrtle Warbler male:* blue-gray upperparts with black streaking; thin, white eye line. *Audubon's Warbler:* similar but with yellow throat. *In flight:* white corners in the tail.
Size: *L* 5½ in; *W* 9¼ in.
Voice: male's song is a brief, bubbling warble rising or falling at the end; much variation between races and individuals; call is a sharp *chip* or *chet*.
Status: common to abundant migrant; uncommon winter resident.
Habitat: a variety of well-vegetated habitats in lowlands, especially in wax myrtle thickets.

Similar Birds

Yellow-throated Warbler

Northern Parula

Magnolia Warbler

Yellow-rumped Warbler 179

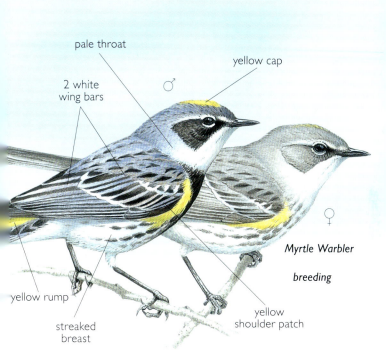

- pale throat
- yellow cap
- 2 white wing bars
- ♂
- ♀
- Myrtle Warbler
- breeding
- yellow rump
- streaked breast
- yellow shoulder patch

Nesting: does not nest in Oklahoma; nests in the western and northern U.S. and in Canada; in a crotch or on a horizontal limb in a conifer; cup nest is made of vegetation and spider silk; brown-blotched, buff-colored eggs are ⅝ x ½ in; female incubates 4–5 eggs for up to 13 days.

Did You Know?

This small warbler's habit of flitting near buildings to snatch spiders from their webs has earned it the nickname "Spider Bird."

Look For

Small puddles that form during or after rains often attract warblers, allowing a glimpse of these secretive birds.

Common Yellowthroat
Geothlypis trichas

The bumblebee colors of the male Common Yellowthroat's black mask and yellow throat identify this skulking wetland resident. He sings his *witchety* song from strategically chosen cattail perches, which he visits in rotation, fiercely guarding his territory against the intrusion of other males. • The Common Yellowthroat is different than most wood-warblers, preferring marshlands and wet, overgrown meadows to forests. The female wears no mask and remains mostly hidden from view in thick vegetation when she tends to the nest.

Other ID: black bill; orangy legs. *Female:* may show faint, white eye ring.
Size: *L* 5 in; *W* 7 in.
Voice: song is a clear, oscillating *witchety witchety witchety-witch;* call is a sharp *tcheck* or *tchet.*
Status: common migrant; uncommon in summer, mostly found in the east; rare in winter.
Habitat: wetlands, riparian areas and wet, overgrown meadows; sometimes dry fields.

Similar Birds

Kentucky Warbler · Wilson's Warbler · Hooded Warbler

Common Yellowthroat

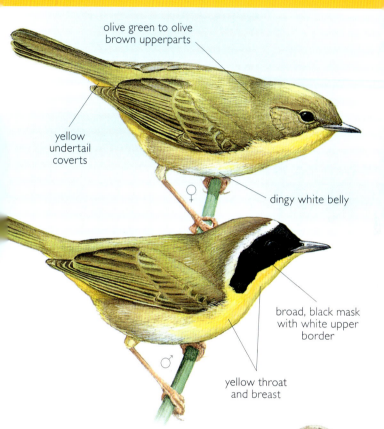

- olive green to olive brown upperparts
- yellow undertail coverts
- dingy white belly
- broad, black mask with white upper border
- yellow throat and breast

Nesting: on or near the ground; often in a small shrub or emergent vegetation; female builds an open cup nest of weeds, grass, bark strips and moss; brown-blotched, white eggs are ⅝ x ½ in; female incubates 3–5 eggs for 12 days.

Did You Know?

Swedish biologist Carolus Linnaeus named the Common Yellowthroat in 1766, making it one of the first North American birds to be described.

Look For

Common Yellowthroats immerse themselves or roll in water, then shake off the excess water by flicking or flapping their wings.

Summer Tanager
Piranga rubra

The Summer Tanager is a treat for Oklahoma birders. This strikingly beautiful bird breeds throughout our forested areas, favoring the edges of forests and riparian areas. • Summer Tanagers thrive on a wide variety of insects, but are best known for snatching flying bees and wasps from menacing swarms. They may even harass the occupants of a wasp nest until the nest is abandoned and the larvae inside are left free for the picking. • The Scarlet Tanager is more restricted to the eastern forests, whereas the Western Tanager is found only in extreme western Oklahoma.

Other ID: *Immature male:* patchy, red and greenish plumage.
Size: *L* 7–8 in; *W* 12 in.
Voice: song is a series of 3–5 sweet, clear, whistled phrases, like a faster version of the American Robin's song; call is *pit* or *pit-a-tuck*.
Status: common summer resident in the eastern half of the state; rare in the west.
Habitat: mixed coniferous and deciduous woodlands, especially those with oak or hickory, or riparian woodlands with cottonwoods; occasionally in wooded backyards.

Similar Birds

Scarlet Tanager Western Tanager Vermilion Flycatcher

Summer Tanager 183

- thick, pale bill
- varies from overall grayish yellow to greenish with reddish wash
- ♀
- small crest
- ♂ rose red overall

Nesting: constructed on a high, horizontal tree limb; female builds a flimsy, shallow cup of grass, Spanish moss and twigs and lines it with fine grass; pale blue-green eggs, spotted with reddish brown are ⅞ x ⅝ in; female incubates 3–4 eggs for 11–12 days.

Did You Know?

A courting male tanager will hop persistently in front of or over the female while offering her food and fanning his handsome crest and tail feathers.

Look For

The male Summer Tanager keeps his rosy red plumage all year, unlike the male Scarlet Tanager, which temporarily molts to a greenish yellow plumage in fall.

Spotted Towhee
Pipilo maculatus

Do not be disappointed if the raccoon you were expecting to see at close range turns out to be a bird slightly smaller than a robin. The Spotted Towhee is capable of quite a ruckus when it forages in loose leaf litter, scraping with both feet. Though confident enough to scold the family cat, the Spotted Towhee is often quite shy and needs to be coaxed out into the open for a good look. It can often be found feeding on the ground beneath a bird feeders during winter, provided there is dense vegetation nearby. • The Eastern Towhee is nearly identical, but lacks the white streaks on its back.

Other ID: white spotting on wings and back; white outer tail corners; white breast and belly; buffy undertail.
Size: *L* 7–8 in; *W* 10–10½ in.
Voice: song is *here here here PLEASE*; distinctive call is a buzzy trill.
Status: common migrant and winter resident; rare summer resident.
Habitat: brushy hedgerows and woods with dense understory; overgrown bushy fields and hillsides; frequently at feeders, especially in winter.

Similar Birds

Eastern Towhee   Canyon Towhee   Dark-eyed Junco, Oregon (p. 200)

Spotted Towhee 185

- red eyes
- black hood, back, wings and tail
- dark, conical bill
- dark rufous sides and flanks

Nesting: low in a shrub or in a depression on the ground; cup of leaves, bark and rootlets is lined with fine grasses and hair; brown-wreathed, white eggs are 1 x ¾ in; pair incubates 3–4 eggs for 12–13 days.

Did You Know?

The closely related Eastern Towhee is found year-round in wooded areas in the eastern third of Oklahoma and is more common during migration.

Look For

Towhees like tangled thickets and overgrown gardens with blackberries and other small fruits, as well as mature woodlands with a blanket of leaf litter on the forest floor.

American Tree Sparrow

Spizella arborea

Most of us know these rufous-capped, spot-breasted sparrows as winter visitors to agricultural fields and backyard feeders. • Although the American Tree Sparrow's name suggests a relationship with trees or forests, it is actually a bird of treeless fields and semi-open, shrubby habitats. It breeds at or above the treeline at northern latitudes, then return to southern Canada and the north-central U.S. to overwinter. Oklahoma hosts large numbers of these birds in late fall and winter.

Other ID: mottled brown upperparts; notched tail; dark legs; dark upper mandible; yellow lower mandible. *Nonbreeding:* gray central crown stripe. *Juvenile:* streaky breast and head.
Size: L 6¼ in; W 9½ in.
Voice: a high, whistled *tseet-tseet* is followed by a short, sweet, musical series of slurred whistles; call is a 3-note *tsee-dle-eat*.
Status: abundant winter resident in the west and central regions; uncommon in southern and eastern Oklahoma.
Habitat: brushy thickets, roadside shrubs, semi-open fields and agricultural croplands.

Similar Birds

Swamp Sparrow

Field Sparrow

American Tree Sparrow 187

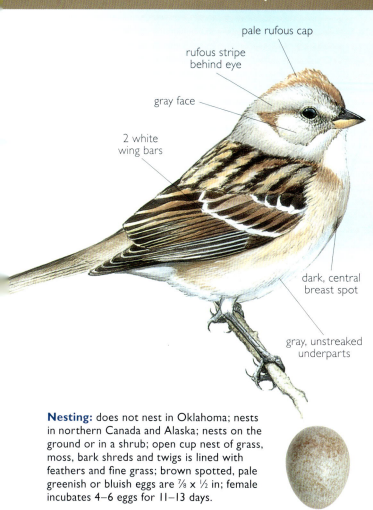

- pale rufous cap
- rufous stripe behind eye
- gray face
- 2 white wing bars
- dark, central breast spot
- gray, unstreaked underparts

Nesting: does not nest in Oklahoma; nests in northern Canada and Alaska; nests on the ground or in a shrub; open cup nest of grass, moss, bark shreds and twigs is lined with feathers and fine grass; brown spotted, pale greenish or bluish eggs are ⅞ x ½ in; female incubates 4–6 eggs for 11–13 days.

Did You Know?

These birds begin courtship in late winter and during spring migration, singing bubbly, bright songs as they move northward.

Look For

These sparrows forage by scratching at the ground for seeds, and they are often seen in mixed flocks with Dark-eyed Juncos.

Sparrows & Buntings

Chipping Sparrow
Spizella passerina

Though the relatively tame Chipping Sparrow sings from a high perch, it commonly nests at eye level, so you can easily watch its breeding and nest-building rituals. You may even participate in the building of this bird's nest by leaving samples of your pet's hair or your own around your backyard. This bird's song is very similar to that of the Dark-eyed Junco. Listen for a slightly faster, drier and less musical series of notes to identify the Chipping Sparrow. • Clay-colored Sparrows are common migrants through central and western Oklahoma.

Other ID: *Breeding:* mottled brown upperparts; light gray, unstreaked underparts; dark bill. *Nonbreeding:* paler crown with dark streaks; brown eyebrow and cheek; pale lower mandible.
Size: *L* 5–6 in; *W* 8½ in.
Voice: song is a rapid, dry trill of *chip* notes; call is a high-pitched *chip*.
Status: common migrant throughout; common summer resident in the east.
Habitat: open conifers or mixed woodland edges; yards and gardens with tree and shrub borders.

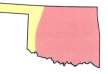

Similar Birds

Field Sparrow

Clay-colored Sparrow

Rufous-crowned Sparrow

Chipping Sparrow 189

- prominent rufous cap
- white eyebrow
- black eye line
- white wing bars

breeding

Nesting: usually at mid-level in a coniferous tree; female builds a cup nest of grass and rootlets lined with hair; pale blue eggs are ¾ x ½ in; female incubates 4 eggs for 11–12 days.

Did You Know?

The Chipping Sparrow is the most common and widely distributed migratory sparrow in North America.

Look For

Chipping Sparrows forage on lawns for the seeds of grasses, dandelions and clovers.

Lark Sparrow
Chondestes grammacus

first winter

The Lark Sparrow's unique, quail-like facial pattern distinguishes it from all other sparrows. This large sparrow is typically seen in open, shrubby areas and edge habitats, but it occasionally ventures into meadows, grassy forest openings and wooded areas. • Courting males are conspicuous and active, singing clear, buzzy trills and spreading their wing and tail feathers. The males will challenge rivals near their nest but do not defend a large territory. • Vespur Sparrows, a common migrant, have a chestnut shoulder patch.

Other ID: white throat, eyebrow and crown stripe; soft brown, mottled back and wings; light-colored legs.
Size: L 6½ in; W 11 in.
Voice: melodious and variable song consists of short trills, buzzes, pauses and clear notes.
Status: common summer resident; rare winter resident.
Habitat: semi-open shrublands, sandhills, sagebrush, golf courses, large lawns and occasionally pastures.

Similar Birds

Vesper Sparrow

Clay-colored Sparrow

Lark Sparrow 191

- chestnut ear patch
- black "mustache" stripe
- pale, unstreaked breast with a central spot
- black tail with white outer tail feathers

Nesting: on the ground or in a low bush; bulky cup nest is made of grass and twigs and lined with finer material; occasionally reuses abandoned thrasher nests; white eggs, marked with dark scrawls or specks, are ¾ x ⅝ in; female incubates 4–5 eggs for 11–13 days.

Did You Know?

The male Lark Sparrow's song reminded early naturalists of the famed Sky Lark of Europe, which served as an inspiration to many poets.

Look For

During migration, these birds are easily identified by their distinct tail pattern as they flush from rural roadsides.

Grasshopper Sparrow
Ammodramus savannarum

The Grasshopper Sparrow is not named for its diet, but rather for its buzzy, insectlike song. Unique among sparrows, the male sings two completely different courtship songs: one ends in a short trill and the other is a prolonged series of high trills that vary in pitch and speed. • They have the best chance of nesting successfully in pastureland, fallow fields or abandoned fields. Nests located along roadsides or in agricultural lands are often destroyed by mowing or harvesting. Populations of this species are declining in much of North America but seem to be relatively stable in Oklahoma.

Other ID: flattened head profile; sharp tail; pale legs; may show small yellow patch on edge of forewing.
Size: *L* 5–5½ in; *W* 7½ in.
Voice: song is a high, faint, buzzy trill preceded by 1–3 high, thin whistled notes: *tea-tea-tea zeeeeeeeeee*.
Status: common summer resident, except in forested regions of southeastern Oklahoma.
Habitat: grasslands and grassy fields with little or no shrub or tree cover.

Similar Birds

Le Conte's Sparrow

Savannah Sparrow

Henslow's Sparrow

Grasshopper Sparrow 193

- pale eye ring
- dark crown with pale central stripe
- small dark spot on buff cheek
- mottled brown and rufous upperparts
- unstreaked, light underparts with buff wash on breast, sides and flanks

Nesting: nests on the ground in tall grass; small cup nest of grass is lined with finer material; white eggs with reddish brown specks are ¾ x ⁹⁄₁₆ in; female incubates 4–5 eggs for 11–13 days.

Did You Know?

The scientific name *Ammodramus* is Greek for "sand runner," while *savannarum* is Latin for "of the savanna," after this bird's grassy, open habitat.

Look For

This tiny, short-tailed sparrow is one of the more common summertime roadside "fence birds" in the grasslands of central Oklahoma.

Song Sparrow
Melospiza melodia

The well-named Song Sparrow is among the great singers of the bird world. When a young male Song Sparrow is only a few months old, he has already created a courtship tune of his own, having learned the basics of melody and rhythm from his father and rival males. • In winter, adaptable Song Sparrows are common throughout Oklahoma and inhabit woodland edges, weedy ditches and riparian thickets. They regularly visit backyard feeders, belting out their sweet, three-part song throughout the year.

Other ID: mottled brown upperparts; rounded tail tip, grayish face.
Size: *L* 6–7 in; *W* 8 in.
Voice: song is 1–4 introductory notes, such as *sweet sweet sweet,* followed by buzzy *towee,* then a short, descending trill; call is short *tsip* or *tchep.*
Status: common winter resident.
Habitat: willow shrublands, riparian thickets, forest openings and pastures, often near water.

Similar Birds

Fox Sparrow

Lincoln's Sparrow

Savannah Sparrow

Song Sparrow 195

- brown line behind eye
- dark crown with pale central stripe
- white jaw line with dark "mustache" stripes
- heavy brown streaks converge at central breast spot

Nesting: does not nest in Oklahoma; nests in central and western U.S., Alaska and Canada; usually on the ground or in a low shrub; female builds an open cup nest of grass, weeds and bark strips; brown-blotched, greenish white eggs are 7/8 x 5/8 in; female incubates 3–5 eggs for 12–14 days.

Did You Know?

Though female songbirds are not usually vocal, the female Song Sparrow will occasionally sing a tune of her own.

Look For

The Song Sparrow pumps its long, rounded tail in flight. It also often issues a high-pitched *seet* flight call.

Harris's Sparrow
Zonotrichia querula

breeding

A wintering Harris's Sparrow has a warm, brown or cinnamon-buff face with variable amounts of black on the throat and upper breast. The size of the black "bib" is controlled by hormones and tends to increase with age, so older males are often the darkest. While "bib" size does not determine rank, body size does, and larger males regularly exert their dominance at roosting and feeding sites.
• The Latin word *querula* means "plaintive" and refers to this bird's quavering, whistled song.

Other ID: *Nonbreeding:* brown face. *Breeding:* black crown, ear patch, throat and "bib"; gray face; black streaks on sides and flanks; white wing bars.
Size: *L* 7–7½ in; *W* 10½ in.
Voice: *jeenk* or *zheenk* call; flocks in flight give a rolling *chug-up chug-up*.
Status: abundant migrant and winter resident in central Oklahoma; uncommon in far eastern and western regions.
Habitat: brushy roadsides, shrubby vegetation, forest edges and riparian thickets.

Similar Birds

Lapland Longspur
(p. 202)

Look For

The Harris's Sparrow is one of the largest sparrows in North America. In winter it often is seen feeding on spilled seeds beneath bird feeders.

Harris's Sparrow

- white flecks on black crown
- pink-orange bill
- mottled, brown and black upperparts
- *nonbreeding*
- brownish sides and flanks
- white underparts

Nesting: does not nest in Oklahoma; nests in the Canadian Arctic; on or near the ground, under a sheltering shrub; open cup nest is made of twigs and plant material; brown-marked, pale green eggs are 7/8 x 5/8 in; female incubates 3–5 eggs over 12–15 days.

Did You Know?

The first nest and eggs of this sparrow were not discovered until 1931, 97 years after the species was first described. The nest with four eggs was found near Churchill, Manitoba, by famous Oklahoma ornithologist George M. Sutton.

White-crowned Sparrow
Zonotrichia leucophrys

Bold and smartly patterned, White-crowned Sparrows brighten brushy hedgerows, overgrown fields and riparian areas in winter. During migration, these sparrows may visit bird feeders stocked with cracked corn. In winter, these sparrows live in flocks and forage mainly for seeds. • The word *Zonotrichia* is Greek for "band" and "hair," a reference to the White-crowned Sparrow's head pattern.

Other ID: gray face, white throat; gray, unstreaked underparts, streaked brown back. *Immature:* head stripes are brown and gray, not black and white.
Size: *L* 5½–7 in; *W* 9½ in.
Voice: several dialects have been identified; song is a highly variable, frequent *I-I-I-got-to-go-wee-wee-now!*; call is a hard *pink* or high *seep*.
Status: common migrant; uncommon in winter; more abundant in western Oklahoma.
Habitat: woodlots, parkland edges, brushy tangles, riparian thickets; also open, weedy fields, lawns and roadsides.

Similar Birds

White-throated Sparrow

Look For

During migration, flocks of these sparrows flit between shrubs, picking seeds from leaf litter and sounding their surprisingly loud, high-pitched *seep* notes.

White-crowned Sparrow 199

- bold, black and white head stripes
- orange-pink bill
- 2 white wing bars

Nesting: does not nest in Oklahoma; in a shrub, small conifer or on the ground; neat cup nest of vegetation is lined with fine materials; darkly marked, blue-green eggs are ⅞ x ⅝ in; female incubates 3–5 eggs 11–14 days.

Did You Know?

Several different races of the White-crowned Sparrow occur in North America, all with similar plumage but different song dialects. Research into this much studied sparrow has given science tremendous insight into bird physiology, homing behavior and the geographic variability of song dialects.

Dark-eyed Junco
Junco hyemalis

Oregon Junco

Juncos usually congregate in backyards with bird feeders and sheltering conifers—with such amenities at their disposal, more and more juncos are appearing in urban areas. These birds spend most of their time on the ground, snatching up seeds beneath bird feeders, and are readily flushed from wooded trails. • Five closely related Dark-eyed Junco subspecies live in North America. The "Slate-colored" and dark-hooded "Oregon" races occur throughout the state, whereas the "Pink-sided," "White-winged" and "Gray-headed" races are only rare winter visitors; the latter two are found almost exclusively in the Panhandle.

Other ID: *Female:* gray-brown where male is slate gray.
Size: *L* 6–7 in; *W* 9 in.
Voice: song is a long, dry trill; call is a smacking *chip* note, often given in series.
Status: abundant winter resident.
Habitat: shrubby woodland borders, backyard feeders.

Similar Birds

Eastern Towhee

Lark Bunting

Dark-eyed Junco 201

- white outer tail feathers
- dark slate gray overall
- pale pink bill
- ♂
- *Slate-Colored Junco*
- white belly and undertail coverts

Nesting: does not breed in Oklahoma; breeds in the northeastern U.S., western U.S., Alaska and Canada; on the ground, usually concealed; female builds a cup nest of twigs, grass, bark shreds and moss; brown-marked, whitish to bluish eggs are ¾ x ½ in; female incubates 3–5 eggs for 12–13 days.

Did You Know?

The junco is often called the "Snow Bird," and the species name, *hyemalis*, means "winter" in Greek.

Look For

This bird flashes its distinctive white outer tail feathers as it rushes for cover.

Lapland Longspur
Calcarius lapponicus

In fall, Lapland Longspurs arrive in Oklahoma. They typically appear wherever open fields offer an abundance of seeds or waste grain. Longspurs can be surprisingly inconspicuous until they are closely approached—then they suddenly erupt into the sky, flashing their white outer tail feathers.
• On several occasions thousands of longspurs have died in a single night from ice storms and other catastrophic weather events. • During blizzards they often burrow beneath the snow, emerging to feed the following morning.

Other ID: *Breeding male:* black crown, face and "bib"; chestnut nape; mottled, brown and black upperparts; broad, white stripe curves down to shoulder from eye (may be tinged with buff behind eye). *Female:* similar to nonbreeding male, but rufous and black areas appear washed out; narrow, lightly streaked, buff breast band.
Size: *L* 6½ in; *W* 11½ in.
Voice: flight calls include a rattled *tri-di-dit* and a descending *teew*.
Status: uncommon winter resident in the east; common to locally abundant winter resident in western Oklahoma.
Habitat: pastures, meadows and croplands.

Similar Birds

Chestnut-collared Longspur

McCown's Longspur

Smith's Longspur

Lapland Longspur

Nesting: does not nest in Oklahoma; nests in the Arctic on open, hummocky tundra; ground nest of grass and sedges is lined with finer material; darkly marked, pale greenish, buff or grayish eggs are 3/4 x 9/16 in; female incubates 4–6 eggs for about 12 days.

Did You Know?

The Lapland Longspur breeds in northern polar regions, including the area of northern Scandinavia known as Lapland.

Look For

Some of the largest concentrations of Lapland Longspurs ever recorded have been in western Oklahoma. Flocks occasionally contain millions of individuals.

Northern Cardinal
Cardinalis cardinalis

The male Northern Cardinal will display his unmistakable, vibrant red head crest and raise his tail when excited or agitated. Famous for defending his territory, he will attack his own reflection in a window, car mirror or even a hubcap! • The Northern Cardinal is one of only a few bird species to maintain strong pair bonds. Some couples sing to each other year-round, while others join loose flocks, reestablishing pair bonds in spring during a "courtship feeding." In this ritual, the male offers a seed to the female, which she then accepts and eats.

Other ID: *Male:* red overall. *Female:* brownish buff overall; fainter mask; red crest, wings and tail.
Size: *L* 8–9 in; *W* 12 in.
Voice: call is a metallic *chip;* song is series of clear, bubbly whistled notes: *What cheer! What cheer! birdie-birdie-birdie what cheer!*
Status: common resident, except in the Panhandle where it is rare.
Habitat: brushy thickets and shrubby tangles along forest and woodland edges; backyards and urban and suburban parks.

Similar Birds

Summer Tanager
(p. 182)

Scarlet Tanager

Rose-breasted Grosbeak

Northern Cardinal 205

- pointed crest
- red, conical bill
- black mask and throat
- ♂
- ♀

Nesting: in a dense shrub or vine tangle or low in a coniferous tree; female builds an open cup nest of twigs, grass and bark shreds; brown-speckled, white to greenish eggs are 1 x ¾ in; female incubates 3–4 eggs for 12–13 days.

Did You Know?

This bird owes its name to the vivid red plumage of the male, which resembles the color of the robes of Roman Catholic cardinals.

Look For

Northern Cardinals fly with jerky movements and short glides. At the feeder they have a preference for sunflower seeds.

Indigo Bunting
Passerina cyanea

The vivid electric blue male Indigo Bunting is one of the more spectacular birds in Oklahoma. This breeder arrives in April or May and favors raspberry thickets as nest sites; the dense thorny stems keep most predators at a distance and the berries are a good food source. • The male is a persistent singer, vocalizing even through the heat of a summer day. A young male doesn't learn his couplet song from his parents, but from neighboring males during his first year on his own. • Planting coneflowers, cosmos or foxtail grasses may attract Indigo Buntings to your backyard.

Other ID: dull gray to blackish legs; no wing bars. *Male:* bright blue overall; black lores. *Female:* soft brown overall; whitish throat.
Size: *L* 5½ in; *W* 8 in.
Voice: song consists of a paired warbled whistles: *fire-fire, where-where, here-here, see-it see-it;* call is a quick *spit*.
Status: common summer resident, except in the Panhandle where it is uncommon.
Habitat: deciduous forest and woodland edges, regenerating forest clearings, orchards and shrubby fields.

Similar Birds

Lazuli Bunting   Blue Grosbeak   Mountain Bluebird

Indigo Bunting 207

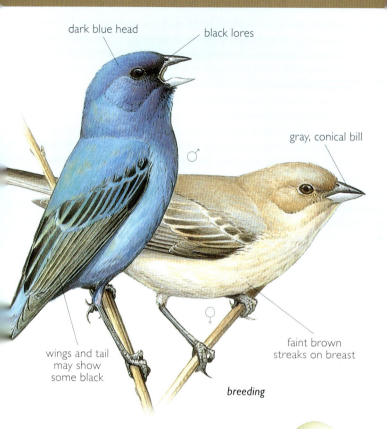

- dark blue head
- black lores
- gray, conical bill
- ♂
- wings and tail may show some black
- ♀
- faint brown streaks on breast

breeding

Nesting: in a small tree, shrub or within a vine tangle; female builds a cup nest of grass, leaves and bark strips; unmarked, white to bluish white eggs are ¾ x ½ in; female incubates 3–4 eggs for 12–13 days.

Did You Know?

Females choose the most melodious males as mates because these males can usually establish territories with the finest habitat.

Look For

The Indigo Bunting will land midway on a stem of grass or a weed and shuffle slowly toward the seed head, bending down the stem to reach the seeds.

Painted Bunting
Passerina ciris

Stunning male Painted Buntings wear almost every color of the rainbow and grace southern thickets with their sweet songs. Although not as unmistakable as the male, the female is still attractive: her plumage is a rich greenish above and pale yellow below. • During the breeding season these birds tend to be very secretive, often spending much of their time in dense foliage. • Unlike some other finches, including Indigo Buntings, adult male Painted Buntings retain their bright colors during winter, which is spent in Central and South America.

Other ID: *Female:* brilliant yellow-green above and pale yellow below; yellow orbital ring. *Juvenile:* similar to female but duller, more grayish green.
Size: *L* 5½ in; *W* 8¾ in.
Voice: song is a sweet, clear series of warbling notes; call is a sharp *chip*.
Status: common summer resident, except in the Panhandle where it is rare.
Habitat: breeds in shrubby fields, hammock edges and citrus groves; may overwinter in backyards with much cover.

Similar Birds

Indigo Bunting
(p. 206)

Blue Grosbeak

Painted Bunting 209

- greenish yellow back and wings
- brilliant blue head with red orbital ring
- red underparts including throat

Nesting: in a shrub or low tree; female weaves an open cup from grass, weed stems and leaves and lines it with fine plant material and animal hair; finely speckled, white eggs are ¾ x ⁹⁄₁₆ in; female incubates 3–4 eggs for 11–12 days; usually double-brooded.

Did You Know?

Painted Buntings have two separate breeding ranges: a larger, mainly inland range and a smaller strip along the Atlantic Coast.

Look For

A breeding male may have multiple mates, but may often find himself caught in violent altercations over territory and breeding privileges.

Dickcissel
Spiza americana

The Dickcissel is one of the summer birds of the Oklahoma countryside, but it may be abundant one year and absent the next. Seeds and grain form the main part of its diet on its South American wintering grounds, making the Dickcissel unpopular with local farmers. Each year large numbers of roosting birds are poisoned in efforts to reduce crop losses, which may partially explain the change in the Dickcissel's population. Because winter flocks can contain over one million birds, targeting a single roost can significantly affect the world population.

Other ID: dark, conical bill; brown upperparts. *Female:* duller version of male; white throat. *Immature:* similar to female but has very faint eyebrow and dark streaking on crown, breast, sides and flanks.
Size: L 6–7 in; W 9½ in.
Voice: song consists of 2–3 single notes followed by a trill, often paraphrased as *dick dick dick-cissel*; flight call is a buzzerlike *bzrrrrt*.
Status: abundant summer resident in central and western Oklahoma; uncommon in eastern Oklahoma.
Habitat: abandoned fields dominated by forbs; weedy meadows, croplands, grasslands and grassy roadsides.

Similar Birds

Eastern Meadowlark

Look For

Breeding males perch atop tall blades of grass, fence posts, telephone wires and sing stuttering, trilled renditions of their own name throughout the day.

Dickcissel 211

breeding

Nesting: on or near the ground; well concealed among tall, dense vegetation; female builds a bulky, open cup nest of grass and other vegetation; pale blue eggs are ⅞ x ⅝ in; female incubates 4 eggs for 11–13 days.

Did You Know?

Dickcissels are polygynous, and males may mate with up to eight females in a single breeding season. Males with better nesting sites in their territory will attract more mates.

Red-winged Blackbird
Agelaius phoeniceus

The male Red-winged Blackbird wears his bright red shoulders like armor—together with his short, raspy song, they are key in defending his territory from rivals. In field experiments, if a male's red shoulders were painted black he soon lost his territory. • Nearly every cattail marsh in Oklahoma hosts Red-winged Blackbirds during at least some of the year. • The female looks like a huge sparrow with a streaked breast. Her cryptic coloration allows her to sit inconspicuously on her nest, blending in perfectly with the surroundings. Brewer's Blackbirds are more common in the west and Rusty Blackbirds are more common in the east.

Other ID: *Male:* black overall. *Female:* mottled brown upperparts; pale eyebrow.
Size: *L* 7½–9 in; *W* 13 in.
Voice: song is a loud, raspy *konk-a-ree* or *ogle-reeeee*; calls include a harsh *check* and high *tseert*; female gives a loud *che-che-che chee chee chee*.
Status: common summer resident; abundant migrant and winter resident.
Habitat: cattail marshes, wet meadows and ditches, croplands and shoreline shrubs.

Similar Birds

Brewer's Blackbird   Rusty Blackbird

Red-winged Blackbird 213

- red shoulder patch edged in yellow
- faint, red shoulder patch
- heavily streaked underparts

Nesting: colonial; in cattails or shoreline bushes; female builds an open cup nest of dried cattail leaves lined with fine grass; darkly marked, pale bluish green eggs are 1 x ¾ in; female incubates 3–4 eggs for 10–12 days.

Did You Know?

Some scientists believe that the Red-winged Blackbird is the most abundant bird species in North America.

Look For

As early as mid-March the male Red-winged Blackbird sings his *konk-a-ree* song and spreads his shoulders to display his bright red wing patch to rivals and potential mates.

Western Meadowlark
Sturnella neglecta

In the early 19th century, members of the Lewis and Clark expedition mistook the Western Meadowlark for the very similar-looking Eastern Meadowlark, hence the scientific name *neglecta*. Where ranges overlap, Western Meadowlarks prefer drier, more barren grasslands, whereas Easterns prefer wetter areas and taller vegetation. The quite dissimilar songs are the easiest and most accurate way to distinguish these species.

Other ID: brown crown stripes and eye line border; pale eyebrow and median crown stripe; yellow lores; long, pinkish legs; short.
Size: L 9–9½ in; W 14½ in.
Voice: song is a rich, melodic series of bubbly, flutelike notes; calls include a low, loud *chuck* or *chup*, a rattling flight call or a few clear whistled notes.
Status: common resident in western Oklahoma, becoming less common eastward.
Habitat: grassy meadows, native prairie and pastures; also in some croplands, weedy fields and grassy roadsides.

Similar Birds

Eastern Meadowlark

Bobolink

Western Meadowlark 215

- mottled brown upperparts
- long, sharp bill
- yellow on throat extends onto lower cheek
- dark streaking on white sides and flanks
- broad, black breast band
- wide tail with white outer tail feathers
- yellow underparts

breeding

Nesting: in a depression or scrape on the ground in dense grass; domed grass nest with side entrance is woven into surrounding vegetation; brown- and purple-spotted, white eggs are 1⅛ x ⅞ in; female incubates 3–7 eggs for 13–15 days.

Did You Know?

Eastern Meadowlarks and Western Meadowlarks may occasionally interbreed, but their offspring are infertile.

Look For

Watch for the Western Meadowlark's courtship dance. Potential partners face each other, raise their bills high in the air and perform a grassland ballet.

Common Grackle
Quiscalus quiscula

The Common Grackle is a poor but spirited singer. While perched in a shrub or tree, a male grackle will slowly take a deep breath to inflate his breast, causing his feathers to spike outward, then close his eyes and give out a loud, strained *tssh-schleek*.
• In fall, large flocks of Common Grackles are found in rural areas. Smaller bands occasionally venture into urban neighborhoods, where they assert their dominance at backyard bird feeders. Because the bird is so common and aggressive, its beautiful bluish black iridescent plumage is not fully appreciated.

Other ID: long, keeled tail; female is smaller, duller and browner than male. *Juvenile:* dull brown overall; dark eyes.
Size: *L* 11–13½ in; *W* 17 in.
Voice: song is a series of harsh, strained notes ending with a metallic squeak: *tssh-schleek* or *gri-de-leeek*; call is a quick, loud *swaaaack* or *chaack*.
Status: common summer resident; uncommon in winter.
Habitat: wetlands, hedgerows, fields, riparian woodlands; also shrubby parks and gardens.

Similar Birds

Great-tailed Grackle

Look For

At night, grackles commonly roost with groups of European Starlings, Red-winged Blackbirds and even Brown-headed Cowbirds.

Common Grackle 217

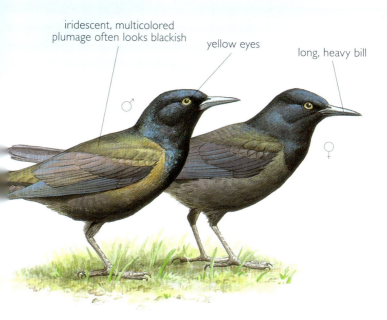

Nesting: singly or in a small colony; in dense tree, shrub or emergent vegetation; often near water; female builds a bulky, open cup nest of twigs, grass, plant fibers and mud and lines it with fine grass or feathers; brown-blotched, pale blue eggs are 1⅛ x ⅞ in; female incubates 4–5 eggs for 12–14 days.

Did You Know?

Compared to other blackbirds the Common Grackle has a long, wedge-shaped tail that trails behind in flight. But its tail is small compared to the enormous tail found on the Great-tailed Grackle, which has expanded northward and is now found locally throughout Oklahoma.

Brown-headed Cowbird
Molothrus ater

These nomads historically followed bison herds across the Great Plains (they now follow cattle), so they never stayed in one area long enough to build and tend a nest. Instead, cowbirds lay their eggs in other birds' nests, relying on the unsuspecting adoptive parents to incubate the eggs and feed the aggressive young. Orioles, warblers, vireos and tanagers are among the most affected species. Increased livestock farming and fragmentation of forests has encouraged the expansion of the cowbird's range. It is known to parasitize more than 140 bird species.

Other ID: dark eyes; thick, conical bill.
Size: *L* 6–8 in; *W* 12 in.
Voice: song is a high, liquidy gurgle: *glug-ahl-whee* or *bubbloozeee;* call is a squeaky, high-pitched *seep, psee* or *wee-tse-tse* or a fast, chipping *ch-ch-ch-ch-ch-ch.*
Status: common migrant and summer resident; uncommon in winter.
Habitat: agricultural and residential areas, usually fields, woodland edges, roadsides.

Similar Birds

Rusty Blackbird   Brewer's Blackbird   Yellow-headed Blackbird

Brown-headed Cowbird

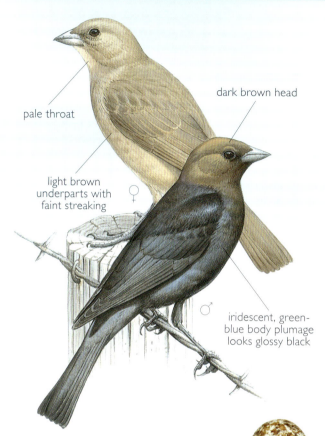

- pale throat
- light brown underparts with faint streaking ♀
- dark brown head
- iridescent, green-blue body plumage looks glossy black ♂

Nesting: does not build a nest; female lays up to 40 eggs a year in the nests of other birds, usually 1 egg per nest; brown-speckled, whitish eggs are ⅞ x ⅝ in; eggs hatch after 10–13 days.

Did You Know?

When courting a female, the male cowbird points his bill upward to the sky, fans his tail and wings and utters a loud *squeek*.

Look For

When cowbirds feed in flocks, they hold their back ends up high, with their tails sticking straight up in the air.

Baltimore Oriole
Icterus galbula

With a flutelike song and a preference for the canopies of neighborhood trees, the Baltimore Oriole is difficult to spot, and a hanging pouch nest dangling in a bare tree in fall is sometimes the only evidence that the bird was there at all. The nests are deceptively strong and often remain intact through the harshest winters. • The planting of trees around farms and in towns has allowed the Baltimore Oriole to expand westward across the formerly treeless plains. However, in extreme western Oklahoma, the Baltimore Oriole is replaced by its western relative, the Bullock's Oriole.

Other ID: *Female:* olive brown upperparts (darkest on head); white wing bar.
Size: *L* 7–8 in; *W* 11½ in.
Voice: song consists of slow, clear whistles: *peter peter peter here peter;* calls include a 2-note *tea-too* and a rapid chatter: *ch-ch-ch-ch-ch.*
Status: common summer resident, less common in southern and western Oklahoma.
Habitat: deciduous and mixed forests, particularly riparian woodlands, natural openings, shorelines, roadsides, orchards, gardens and parklands.

Similar Birds

Orchard Oriole   Bullock's Oriole   Black-headed Grosbeak

Baltimore Oriole 221

- black hood, back, wings and central tail feathers
- thick, orange wing bar
- dull yellow-orange underparts and rump
- bright orange underparts, shoulder, rump and outer tail feathers
- white wing patch and feather edgings

Nesting: high in a deciduous tree; female builds a hanging pouch nest of grass, bark shreds and grapevines; darkly marked, pale gray to bluish white eggs are ⅞ x ⅝ in; female incubates 4–5 eggs for 12–14 days.

Did You Know?

The male's plumage mirror the colors of the coat of arms of Sir George Calvert, Baron of Baltimore, who established the first colony in Maryland.

Look For

In fall, you can sometimes see a Baltimore Oriole in its Halloween colors at a feeder, especially if orange halves or grape jelly are offered.

House Finch
Carpodacus mexicanus

A native to western North America, the House Finch was brought to eastern parts of the continent as an illegally captured cage bird known as the "Hollywood Finch." In the early 1940s, New York pet shop owners released their birds to avoid prosecution and fines, and it is likely the descendants of those birds colonized the eastern U.S. Meanwhile, House Finches were also expanding across Oklahoma from the west. The two populations were reunited here in the late 1980s and early 1990s. The House Finch is now commonly found throughout the continental U.S. and has been introduced in Hawaii.

Other ID: streaked undertail coverts.
Female: indistinct facial patterning; heavily streaked underparts.
Size: *L* 5–6 in; *W* 9½ in.
Voice: song is a bright, disjointed warble lasting about 3 seconds, often ending with a harsh *jeeer* or *wheer*; flight call is a sweet *cheer*, given singly or in series.
Status: common resident.
Habitat: cities, towns and agricultural areas.

Similar Birds

Purple Finch

Red Crossbill

Rose-breasted Grosbeak

House Finch

Nesting: in a cavity, building, dense foliage or abandoned bird nest; open cup nest of plants and other debris; pale blue, spotted eggs are ¾ x ⁹⁄₁₆ in; female incubates 4–5 eggs for 12–14 days.

Did You Know?

The male House Finch's plumage varies in color from light yellow to bright red, but females will choose the reddest males with which to breed.

Look For

In flight, the House Finch has a square tail whereas the similar-looking Purple Finch has a sharply notched tail.

Pine Siskin
Carduelis pinus

Pine Siskins are unpredictable, social birds that may be abundant for a time, then suddenly disappear. Since their favored habitats are widely scattered, flocks are constantly on the move, searching forests for the most lucrative seed crops. These drab, sparrowlike birds are easy to overlook at first, but once you recognize their characteristic rising *zzzreeeee* calls and boisterous chatter, you will encounter them with surprising frequency. They often feed near the treetops, favoring coniferous and mixed woodlands and forest edges. They also visit bird feeders, especially thistle feeders.

Other ID: dull wing bars; indistinct facial pattern.
Size: *L* 4½–5½ in; *W* 9 in.
Voice: song is a variable, bubbly mix of squeaky, raspy, metallic notes, sometimes resembling a jerky laugh; call is a buzzy, rising *zzzreeeee*.
Status: common migrant and winter resident.
Habitat: Coniferous and mixed forests; parks, cemeteries and residential areas, especially if pines are present.

Similar Birds

Common Redpoll   Purple Finch   House Finch

Pine Siskin

- dark, heavily streaked upperparts
- heavily streaked underparts
- yellow highlights at base of tail feathers and on wings (easily seen in flight)
- slightly forked tail

Nesting: does not nest in Oklahoma; nests in the western states and across Canada; usually loosely colonial; typically on an outer branch of a conifer; female builds a loose cup nest of twigs and grass, lined with finer material; darkly spotted, pale blue eggs are ⅝ x ½ in; female incubates 3–5 eggs for about 13 days.

Did You Know?

Pine Siskins are attracted to road salts, mineral licks and ashes, all of which add minerals to their diet.

Look For

The best way to meet these birds is to set up a finch feeder filled with black niger seed in your backyard and wait for them to appear.

American Goldfinch
Carduelis tristis

nonbreeding

Like vibrant rays of sunshine, American Goldfinches cheerily flutter over weedy fields, gardens and along roadsides. It is hard to miss their call and their distinctive, undulating style of flight. • Because these acrobatic birds regularly feed while hanging upside down, finch feeders are designed with the seed openings below the perches. Use niger or black-oil sunflower seeds to attract American Goldfinches to your bird feeder. • Lesser Goldfinches are occasionally seen, mostly in far western Oklahoma.

Other ID: *Female:* yellow throat and breast; yellow-green belly. *Nonbreeding male:* olive brown back; yellow-tinged head; gray underparts.
Size: L 4½–5 in; W 9 in.
Voice: song is a long, varied series of trills, twitters, warbles and hissing notes; calls include *po-ta-to-chip* or *per-chic-or-ee* (often delivered in flight) and a whistled *dear-me, see-me*.
Status: common winter resident; uncommon summer resident.
Habitat: weedy fields, woodland edges, meadows, riparian areas, parks and gardens.

Similar Birds

Evening Grosbeak

Wilson's Warbler

Lesser Goldfinch

American Goldfinch

breeding

Nesting: in a fork of a deciduous tree; compact cup nest is made of plant fibers, grass and spider silk; pale bluish, spotted eggs are ⅝ x ½ in; female incubates 4–6 eggs for 12–14 days.

Did You Know?

These birds nest in late summer to ensure that there is a dependable source of seeds from thistles and dandelions to feed their young.

Look For

American Goldfinches delight in perching on late-summer thistle heads or poking through dandelion patches in search of seeds.

House Sparrow
Passer domesticus

This abundant and conspicuous bird was introduced to North America in the 1850s as part of a plan to control the insects that were damaging grain and cereal crops. As it turns out, these birds are largely vegetarian! • The House Sparrow's tendency to usurp territory has led to a decline in native bird populations. This sparrow will even help itself to the convenience of another bird's home, such as a bluebird or Cliff Swallow nest or a Purple Martin house. • This bird is not a true sparrow, but an Old World weaver finch.

Other ID: *Breeding male:* gray crown; black bill; dark, mottled upperparts; gray underparts; white wing bar. *Female:* indistinct facial pattern; plain gray-brown overall; streaked upperparts.
Size: *L* 5½–6½ in; *W* 9½ in.
Voice: song is a plain, familiar *cheep-cheep-cheep-cheep;* call is a short *chill-up.*
Status: common year-round resident.
Habitat: townsites, urban and suburban areas, farmyards and agricultural areas, railroad yards and other developed areas.

Similar Birds

Harris's Sparrow
(p. 196)

Look For

In spring, House Sparrows feast on the buds of fruit trees. In winter, they flock around farm buildings in rural areas and at garbage dumps in towns and cities.

House Sparrow 229

- buffy eyebrow
- chestnut nape
- black lore and "bib"
- light gray cheek

♀

♂

breeding

Nesting: often communal; in a human-made structure, ornamental shrub or natural cavity; pair builds a large dome nest of grass, twigs and plant fibers; gray-speckled, white to greenish eggs are 7/8 x 5/8 in; pair incubates 4–6 eggs for 10–13 days.

Did You Know?

The House Sparrow has successfully established itself in North America in part because of its high reproductive output. A pair may raise up to four clutches per year, with up to eight young per clutch.

Glossary

brood: *n.* a family of young from one hatching; v. to sit on eggs so as to hatch them.

buteo: a high-soaring hawk (genus *Buteo*); characterized by broad wings and short, wide tails; feeds mostly on small mammals and other land animals.

cere: a fleshy area at the base of a bird's bill that contains the nostrils.

clutch: the number of eggs laid by the female at one time.

corvid: a member of the crow family (Corvidae); includes crows, jays, ravens and magpies.

crop: an enlargement of the esophagus; serves as a storage structure and (in pigeons) has glands that produce secretions.

dabbling: a foraging technique used by ducks, in which the head and neck are submerged but the body and tail remain on the water's surface; dabbling ducks can usually walk easily on land, can take off without running and have brightly colored speculums.

eclipse plumage: a cryptic plumage, similar to that of females, worn by some male ducks in fall when they molt their flight feathers and consequently are unable to fly.

endangered: a species that is facing extirpation or extinction in all or part of its range.

extirpated: a species that no longer exists in the wild in a particular region but occurs elsewhere.

fledge: to leave the nest for the first time.

fledgling: a young bird that has left the nest but is dependent upon its parents.

flushing: a behavior in which frightened birds explode into flight in response to a disturbance.

flycatching: a feeding behavior in which the bird leaves a perch, snatches an insect in midair and returns to the same perch.

hawking: attempting to catch insects through aerial pursuit.

leading edge: the front edge of the wing as viewed from below.

mantle: feathers of the back and upperside of folded wings.

molt: the periodic shedding and regrowth of worn feathers (often twice per year).

morph: one of several alternate plumages displayed by members of a species.

primaries: the outermost flight feathers.

riparian: refers to habitat along riverbanks.

rufous: rusty red in color.

speculum: a brightly colored patch on the wings of many dabbling ducks.

vagrant: a transient bird found outside its normal range.

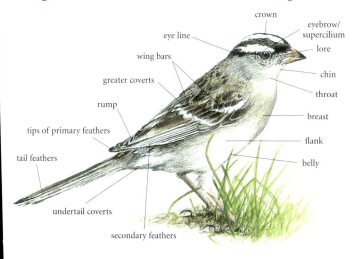

Checklist

The following checklist contains 470 species that have been officially recorded in Oklahoma. Species are grouped by family and listed in taxonomic order in accordance with the A.O.U. *Check-list of North American Birds* (7th ed.) and its supplements.

Accidental and casual species are in italics. In addition, the following risk categories identified by the Oklahoma Department of Wildlife Conservation are also noted: extinct (ex), endangered (en), threatened (th) and of special concern (sc).

We wish to thank the Oklahoma Bird Records Committee for their kind assistance in providing the information for this checklist.

Waterfowl
- ❏ Black-bellied Whistling-Duck
- ❏ Fulvous Whistling-Duck
- ❏ Greater White-fronted Goose
- ❏ Snow Goose
- ❏ Ross's Goose
- ❏ Brant
- ❏ Barnacle Goose
- ❏ Cackling Goose
- ❏ Canada Goose
- ❏ *Mute Swan*
- ❏ Trumpeter Swan
- ❏ Tundra Swan
- ❏ Wood Duck
- ❏ Gadwall
- ❏ Eurasian Wigeon
- ❏ American Wigeon
- ❏ American Black Duck
- ❏ Mallard
- ❏ Mottled Duck
- ❏ Blue-winged Teal
- ❏ Cinnamon Teal
- ❏ Northern Shoveler
- ❏ Northern Pintail
- ❏ Garganey
- ❏ *Baikal Teal*
- ❏ Green-winged Teal
- ❏ Canvasback
- ❏ Redhead
- ❏ Ring-necked Duck
- ❏ Greater Scaup
- ❏ Lesser Scaup
- ❏ Surf Scoter
- ❏ White-winged Scoter
- ❏ Black Scoter
- ❏ Long-tailed Duck
- ❏ Bufflehead
- ❏ Common Goldeneye
- ❏ Barrow's Goldeneye
- ❏ Hooded Merganser
- ❏ Common Merganser
- ❏ Red-breasted Merganser
- ❏ Ruddy Duck

Grouse & Allies
- ❏ Ring-necked Pheasant
- ❏ *Gunnison Sage-Grouse*
- ❏ *Sharp-tailed Grouse*
- ❏ Greater Prairie-Chicken
- ❏ Lesser Prairie-Chicken
- ❏ Wild Turkey

Quails
- ❏ Scaled Quail
- ❏ Northern Bobwhite

Loons
- ❏ Red-throated Loon
- ❏ Pacific Loon
- ❏ Common Loon
- ❏ Yellow-billed Loon

Grebes
- ❏ Least Grebe
- ❏ Pied-billed Grebe
- ❏ Horned Grebe
- ❏ Red-necked Grebe
- ❏ Eared Grebe
- ❏ Western Grebe
- ❏ Clark's Grebe

Gannets
- ❏ Northern Gannet

Pelicans
- ❏ American White Pelican
- ❏ Brown Pelican

Cormorants
- ❏ Neotropic Cormorant
- ❏ Double-crested Cormorant

Darters
- ❏ Anhinga

Frigatebirds
- ❏ Magnificent Frigatebird
- ❏ Great Frigatebird

Herons
- ❏ American Bittern
- ❏ Least Bittern
- ❏ Great Blue Heron
- ❏ Great Egret
- ❏ Snowy Egret
- ❏ Little Blue Heron
- ❏ Tricolored Heron
- ❏ Reddish Egret
- ❏ Cattle Egret
- ❏ Green Heron
- ❏ Black-crowned Night-Heron
- ❏ Yellow-crowned Night-Heron

Ibises & Spoonbills
- ❏ White Ibis
- ❏ Glossy Ibis
- ❏ White-faced Ibis
- ❏ Roseate Spoonbill

Storks
- ❏ Jabiru
- ❏ Wood Stork

Vultures
- ❏ Black Vulture
- ❏ Turkey Vulture

Kites, Hawks & Eagles
- ❏ Osprey
- ❏ Swallow-tailed Kite
- ❏ White-tailed Kite
- ❏ Mississippi Kite
- ❏ Bald Eagle (th)
- ❏ Northern Harrier
- ❏ Sharp-shinned Hawk
- ❏ Cooper's Hawk
- ❏ Northern Goshawk
- ❏ Harris's Hawk
- ❏ Red-shouldered Hawk
- ❏ Broad-winged Hawk
- ❏ *Gray Hawk*
- ❏ Swainson's Hawk (sc)
- ❏ Red-tailed Hawk
- ❏ Ferruginous Hawk (sc)
- ❏ Rough-legged Hawk
- ❏ Golden Eagle (sc)

Falcons
- ❏ Crested Caracara
- ❏ American Kestrel
- ❏ Merlin
- ❏ Gyrfalcon
- ❏ Peregrine Falcon
- ❏ Prairie Falcon (sc)

Rails, Gallinules & Coots
- ❏ Yellow Rail
- ❏ Black Rail
- ❏ King Rail
- ❏ Virginia Rail
- ❏ Sora
- ❏ Purple Gallinule
- ❏ Common Moorhen
- ❏ American Coot

Cranes
- ❏ Sandhill Crane
- ❏ Whooping Crane (en)

Plovers
- ❏ Black-bellied Plover
- ❏ American Golden-Plover
- ❏ Snowy Plover (sc)
- ❏ Wilson's Plover
- ❏ Semipalmated Plover
- ❏ Piping Plover (th)
- ❏ Killdeer
- ❏ Mountain Plover (sc)

Stilts & Avocets
- ❏ Black-necked Stilt
- ❏ American Avocet

Sandpipers & Allies
- ❏ Spotted Sandpiper
- ❏ Solitary Sandpiper
- ❏ Greater Yellowlegs
- ❏ Willet
- ❏ Lesser Yellowlegs
- ❏ Upland Sandpiper
- ❏ Eskimo Curlew (ex)
- ❏ Whimbrel
- ❏ Long-billed Curlew (sc)
- ❏ Hudsonian Godwit
- ❏ Marbled Godwit
- ❏ Ruddy Turnstone
- ❏ Red Knot
- ❏ Sanderling
- ❏ Semipalmated Sandpiper
- ❏ Western Sandpiper
- ❏ Least Sandpiper
- ❏ White-rumped Sandpiper
- ❏ Baird's Sandpiper
- ❏ Pectoral Sandpiper
- ❏ Purple Sandpiper
- ❏ Dunlin
- ❏ *Curlew Sandpiper*
- ❏ Stilt Sandpiper
- ❏ Buff-breasted Sandpiper
- ❏ Ruff
- ❏ Short-billed Dowitcher
- ❏ Long-billed Dowitcher
- ❏ Wilson's Snipe
- ❏ American Woodcock
- ❏ Wilson's Phalarope
- ❏ Red-necked Phalarope
- ❏ Red Phalarope

Gulls & Allies
- ❏ Laughing Gull
- ❏ Franklin's Gull
- ❏ Little Gull
- ❏ Black-headed Gull
- ❏ Bonaparte's Gull
- ❏ Heermann's Gull
- ❏ Mew Gull
- ❏ Ring-billed Gull
- ❏ California Gull
- ❏ Herring Gull
- ❏ Thayer's Gull
- ❏ Iceland Gull
- ❏ Lesser Black-backed Gull
- ❏ Glaucous-winged Gull
- ❏ Glaucous Gull
- ❏ Great Black-backed Gull
- ❏ Sabine's Gull
- ❏ Black-legged Kittiwake
- ❏ Least Tern (en)
- ❏ Caspian Tern
- ❏ Black Tern
- ❏ Common Tern
- ❏ Arctic Tern
- ❏ Forster's Tern
- ❏ Royal Tern
- ❏ Black Skimmer

Jaegers
- ❏ Pomarine Jaeger
- ❏ Parasitic Jaeger

Pigeons & Doves
- ❏ Rock Pigeon
- ❏ Band-tailed Pigeon
- ❏ Eurasian Collared-Dove
- ❏ White-winged Dove
- ❏ Mourning Dove
- ❏ Passenger Pigeon (ex)
- ❏ Inca Dove
- ❏ Common Ground-Dove

Parakeets
- ❏ *Monk Parakeet*
- ❏ Carolina Parakeet (ex)

Cuckoos & Allies
- ❏ Yellow-billed Cuckoo
- ❏ Black-billed Cuckoo
- ❏ Greater Roadrunner
- ❏ Groove-billed Ani

Owls
- ❏ Barn Owl (sc)
- ❏ Western Screech-Owl
- ❏ Eastern Screech-Owl
- ❏ Great Horned Owl
- ❏ Snowy Owl
- ❏ Burrowing Owl (sc)
- ❏ Barred Owl
- ❏ Long-eared Owl
- ❏ Short-eared Owl
- ❏ Northern Saw-whet Owl

Nightjars
- ❏ Lesser Nighthawk
- ❏ Common Nighthawk

- ❏ Common Poorwill
- ❏ Chuck-will's-widow
- ❏ Whip-poor-will

Swifts
- ❏ Chimney Swift
- ❏ *White-throated Swift*

Hummingbirds
- ❏ Green Violet-ear
- ❏ Broad-billed Hummingbird
- ❏ Ruby-throated Hummingbird
- ❏ Black-chinned Hummingbird
- ❏ Anna's Hummingbird
- ❏ Calliope Hummingbird
- ❏ Broad-tailed Hummingbird
- ❏ Rufous Hummingbird

Kingfishers
- ❏ Ringed Kingfisher
- ❏ Belted Kingfisher

Woodpeckers
- ❏ Lewis's Woodpecker
- ❏ Red-headed Woodpecker
- ❏ Acorn Woodpecker
- ❏ Golden-fronted Woodpecker
- ❏ Red-bellied Woodpecker
- ❏ Williamson's Sapsucker
- ❏ Yellow-bellied Sapsucker
- ❏ Red-naped Sapsucker
- ❏ Ladder-backed Woodpecker
- ❏ Downy Woodpecker
- ❏ Hairy Woodpecker
- ❏ Red-cockaded Woodpecker (en)
- ❏ Northern Flicker
- ❏ Pileated Woodpecker
- ❏ Ivory-billed Woodpecker (ex)

Flycatchers
- ❏ Olive-sided Flycatcher
- ❏ Western Wood-Pewee
- ❏ Eastern Wood-Pewee
- ❏ Yellow-bellied Flycatcher
- ❏ Acadian Flycatcher
- ❏ Alder Flycatcher
- ❏ Willow Flycatcher
- ❏ Least Flycatcher
- ❏ Hammond's Flycatcher
- ❏ *Gray Flycatcher*
- ❏ Dusky Flycatcher
- ❏ Cordilleran Flycatcher
- ❏ Black Phoebe
- ❏ Eastern Phoebe
- ❏ Say's Phoebe
- ❏ Vermilion Flycatcher
- ❏ *Dusky-capped Flycatcher*
- ❏ Ash-throated Flycatcher
- ❏ Great Crested Flycatcher
- ❏ Great Kiskadee
- ❏ Cassin's Kingbird
- ❏ Western Kingbird
- ❏ Eastern Kingbird
- ❏ Scissor-tailed Flycatcher

Shrikes
- ❏ Loggerhead Shrike (sc)
- ❏ Northern Shrike

Vireos
- ❏ White-eyed Vireo
- ❏ Bell's Vireo (sc)
- ❏ Black-capped Vireo (en)
- ❏ Gray Vireo
- ❏ Yellow-throated Vireo
- ❏ Plumbeous Vireo
- ❏ Cassin's Vireo
- ❏ Blue-headed Vireo
- ❏ Warbling Vireo
- ❏ Philadelphia Vireo
- ❏ Red-eyed Vireo

Jays & Crows
- ❏ *Gray Jay*
- ❏ Steller's Jay
- ❏ Blue Jay
- ❏ Western Scrub-Jay
- ❏ Pinyon Jay
- ❏ Clark's Nutcracker
- ❏ Black-billed Magpie
- ❏ American Crow
- ❏ Fish Crow
- ❏ Chihuahuan Raven
- ❏ Common Raven

Larks
- ❏ Horned Lark

Swallows
- ❏ Purple Martin
- ❏ Tree Swallow
- ❏ *Violet-green Swallow*
- ❏ Northern Rough-winged Swallow
- ❏ Bank Swallow

- ❏ Cliff Swallow
- ❏ *Cave Swallow*
- ❏ Barn Swallow

Chickadees & Titmice
- ❏ Carolina Chickadee
- ❏ Black-capped Chickadee
- ❏ Mountain Chickadee
- ❏ Juniper Titmouse
- ❏ Tufted Titmouse
- ❏ Black-crested Titmouse
- ❏ Verdin
- ❏ Bushtit

Nuthatches
- ❏ Red-breasted Nuthatch
- ❏ White-breasted Nuthatch
- ❏ Pygmy Nuthatch
- ❏ Brown-headed Nuthatch

Creepers
- ❏ Brown Creeper

Wrens
- ❏ Rock Wren
- ❏ Canyon Wren
- ❏ Carolina Wren
- ❏ Bewick's Wren
- ❏ House Wren
- ❏ Winter Wren
- ❏ Sedge Wren
- ❏ Marsh Wren

Kinglets
- ❏ Golden-crowned Kinglet
- ❏ Ruby-crowned Kinglet

Gnatcatchers
- ❏ Blue-gray Gnatcatcher

Thrushes
- ❏ Eastern Bluebird
- ❏ Western Bluebird
- ❏ Mountain Bluebird
- ❏ Townsend's Solitaire
- ❏ Veery
- ❏ Gray-cheeked Thrush
- ❏ Swainson's Thrush
- ❏ Hermit Thrush
- ❏ Wood Thrush
- ❏ American Robin
- ❏ Varied Thrush

Mockingbirds & Thrashers
- ❏ Gray Catbird
- ❏ Northern Mockingbird
- ❏ Sage Thrasher
- ❏ Brown Thrasher
- ❏ Curve-billed Thrasher

Starlings
- ❏ European Starling

Wagtails & Pipits
- ❏ American Pipit
- ❏ Sprague's Pipit

Waxwings
- ❏ Bohemian Waxwing
- ❏ Cedar Waxwing

Silky-flycatchers
- ❏ *Phainopepla*

Wood-warblers
- ❏ Blue-winged Warbler
- ❏ Golden-winged Warbler
- ❏ Tennessee Warbler
- ❏ Orange-crowned Warbler
- ❏ Nashville Warbler
- ❏ Virginia's Warbler
- ❏ Northern Parula
- ❏ Yellow Warbler
- ❏ Chestnut-sided Warbler
- ❏ Magnolia Warbler
- ❏ Cape May Warbler
- ❏ Black-throated Blue Warbler
- ❏ Yellow-rumped Warbler
- ❏ Black-throated Gray Warbler
- ❏ Black-throated Green Warbler
- ❏ Townsend's Warbler
- ❏ Blackburnian Warbler
- ❏ Yellow-throated Warbler
- ❏ *Grace's Warbler*
- ❏ Pine Warbler
- ❏ Prairie Warbler
- ❏ Palm Warbler
- ❏ Bay-breasted Warbler
- ❏ Blackpoll Warbler
- ❏ Cerulean Warbler
- ❏ Black-and-white Warbler
- ❏ American Redstart
- ❏ Prothonotary Warbler
- ❏ Worm-eating Warbler

- ❏ Swainson's Warbler
- ❏ Ovenbird
- ❏ Northern Waterthrush
- ❏ Louisiana Waterthrush
- ❏ Kentucky Warbler
- ❏ Connecticut Warbler
- ❏ Mourning Warbler
- ❏ MacGillivray's Warbler
- ❏ Common Yellowthroat
- ❏ Hooded Warbler
- ❏ Wilson's Warbler
- ❏ Canada Warbler
- ❏ Yellow-breasted Chat

Tanagers
- ❏ Summer Tanager
- ❏ Scarlet Tanager
- ❏ Western Tanager

Sparrows & Allies
- ❏ Green-tailed Towhee
- ❏ Spotted Towhee
- ❏ Eastern Towhee
- ❏ Canyon Towhee
- ❏ Cassin's Sparrow
- ❏ Bachman's Sparrow (sc)
- ❏ Rufous-crowned Sparrow
- ❏ American Tree Sparrow
- ❏ Chipping Sparrow
- ❏ Clay-colored Sparrow
- ❏ Brewer's Sparrow
- ❏ Field Sparrow
- ❏ Vesper Sparrow
- ❏ Lark Sparrow
- ❏ Black-throated Sparrow
- ❏ Sage Sparrow
- ❏ Lark Bunting
- ❏ Savannah Sparrow
- ❏ Grasshopper Sparrow
- ❏ Baird's Sparrow
- ❏ Henslow's Sparrow
- ❏ Le Conte's Sparrow
- ❏ Nelson's Sharp-tailed Sparrow
- ❏ Fox Sparrow
- ❏ Song Sparrow
- ❏ Lincoln's Sparrow
- ❏ Swamp Sparrow
- ❏ White-throated Sparrow
- ❏ Harris's Sparrow
- ❏ White-crowned Sparrow
- ❏ Dark-eyed Junco
- ❏ McCown's Longspur
- ❏ Lapland Longspur
- ❏ Smith's Longspur
- ❏ Chestnut-collared Longspur

Grosbeaks & Buntings
- ❏ Snow Bunting
- ❏ Northern Cardinal
- ❏ Pyrrhuloxia
- ❏ Rose-breasted Grosbeak
- ❏ Black-headed Grosbeak
- ❏ Blue Grosbeak
- ❏ Lazuli Bunting
- ❏ Indigo Bunting
- ❏ Painted Bunting
- ❏ Dickcissel

Blackbirds & Allies
- ❏ Bobolink
- ❏ Red-winged Blackbird
- ❏ Eastern Meadowlark
- ❏ Western Meadowlark
- ❏ Yellow-headed Blackbird
- ❏ Rusty Blackbird
- ❏ Brewer's Blackbird
- ❏ Common Grackle
- ❏ Great-tailed Grackle
- ❏ Shiny Cowbird
- ❏ *Bronzed Cowbird*
- ❏ Brown-headed Cowbird
- ❏ Orchard Oriole
- ❏ Bullock's Oriole
- ❏ Baltimore Oriole

Finches
- ❏ Pine Grosbeak
- ❏ Purple Finch
- ❏ Cassin's Finch
- ❏ House Finch
- ❏ Red Crossbill
- ❏ White-winged Crossbill
- ❏ Common Redpoll
- ❏ Pine Siskin
- ❏ Lesser Goldfinch
- ❏ American Goldfinch
- ❏ Evening Grosbeak

Old World Sparrows
- ❏ House Sparrow

Index

A

Accipiter cooperii, 66
Actitis macularius, 78
Agelaius phoeniceus, 212
Aix sponsa, 24
Ammodramus savannarum, 192
Anas
    discors, 30
    platyrhynchos, 28
    strepera, 26
Archilochus colubris, 110
Ardea
    alba, 54
    herodias, 52
Aythya
    affinis, 34
    americana, 32

B

Baeolophus bicolor, 150
Blackbird, Red-winged, 212
Bluebird, Eastern, 160
Bobwhite, Northern, 44
Bombycilla cedrorum, 172
Branta canadensis, 22
Bubo virginianus, 102
Bucephala clangula, 36
Bunting,
    Indigo, 206
    Painted, 208
Buteo
    jamaicensis, 70
    swainsoni, 68

C

Calcarius lapponicus, 202
Calidris bairdii, 82
Cardinal, Northern, 204
Cardinalis cardinalis, 204
Carduelis
    pinus, 224
    tristis, 226
Carpodacus mexicanus, 222
Catbird, Gray, 164
Cathartes aura, 58
Ceryle alcyon, 112
Chaetura pelagica, 108
Charadrius vociferus, 76

Chen caerulescens, 20
Chickadee, Carolina, 148
Chondestes grammacus, 190
Chordeiles minor, 106
Circus cyaneus, 64
Coccyzus americanus, 96
Colaptes auratus, 120
Colinus virginianus, 44
Collared-Dove, Eurasian, 92
Columba livia, 90
Coot, American, 74
Cormorant, Double-crested, 50
Corvus brachyrhynchos, 138
Cowbird, Brown-headed, 218
Crow, American, 138
Cuckoo, Yellow-billed, 96
Cyanocitta cristata, 136

D

Dendroica
    coronata, 178
    petechia, 176
Dickcissel, 210
Dove, Mourning, 94
Duck, Wood, 24
Dumetella carolinensis, 164

E

Eagle, Bald, 62
Egret, Great, 54
Empidonax minimus, 122
Eremophila alpestris, 140

F

Falco sparverius, 72
Finch, House, 222
Flicker, Northern, 120
Flycatcher,
    Great Crested, 126
    Least, 122
    Scissor-tailed, 132
Forster's Tern, 88
Fulica americana, 74

G

Gadwall, 26
Geococcyx californianus, 98
Geothlypis trichas, 180